This book is designed for use on a weekly basis, to provide employees with foundational safety knowledge of their job. The topics provided here are specific to lawncare.

We are providing 60 topics for 1year, as some workplaces may not find all topics 100% applicable, or this allows to reuse this book every year and not always have the same topics.

No matter how you use this book, hopefully you find it helpful to improving safety in your workplace.

Toolbox Talks for Lawncare

Table of Content

Delivering Your Toolbox Talk

Worker safety should always be the number one priority of every company. Toolbox talks should be conducted on a regular basis to educate workers on safe work practices and stay compliant with regulations regarding safety and training.

Safety toolbox talks are important to building a strong safety culture and reinforcing your company's commitment to protecting your workers. Holding toolbox talks can prevent workers from getting complacent and avoid taking safety for granted.

Conduct toolbox talks on a monthly basis to reinforce your company's focus on safety. Toolbox talks, sometimes referred to as tailgate meetings or safety briefings, are short, informal safety meetings held at the start of a day or shift.

Toolbox talks are a great way to reinforce safety basics, focus on high-risk scenarios and to inform workers about changes to the job and/or working conditions that may have occurred. Be sure to discuss any accidents or injuries that have occurred and how they could have been prevented.

These simple tips can help you in your toolbox talk delivery:

Practice makes perfect

Yes, it's a cliché - but it's true. If you want to communicate a subject well, you need to know it well yourself. Reading off a script will not hold the attention of your audience, so get to know the presentation, read through it a few times, familiarise yourself with the format and structure of the talk you want to deliver.

Practice first and your talk will go much smoother - the more you do, the less you will need to practice.

Stay on topic

Try not to get sidetracked by other subjects or topics. Toolbox talks should focus on one subject, if there is another important subject that comes up and it doesn't require immediate attention, use it as the subject for your next toolbox talk. If it does require urgent attention, finish your toolbox talk, and address the issue afterwards.

If you try to cover more than one topic or too much in a talk, then the delivery will be diluted, and the message could get lost in the middle.

Pace yourself

You need to keep your audience's attention with a short, direct toolbox talk - but that doesn't mean you should rush what you are saying. Monitor the speed at which you are talking and keep at a nice steady pace.

It's better to deliver just the important information in a clear way, rather than try to rush through lots of information that gets forgotten.

Keep it simple

Avoid jargon and make sure your talk is easy to follow. Break the subject down into key sections, for example, an introduction, key points and key safety measures.

Use simple words and phrases and try to avoid technical language - or explain if you do need to use it.

Consider new or inexperienced workers, also give consideration to workers where English is not their first language.

Present positively

If you want others to be interested in what you have to say, you need to be interested in what you have to say. Show enthusiasm for the topic, you should aim to deliver a clear message and get your workers to understand the importance of good health and safety practices on site.

People will be more inclined to listen to a positive talk, and the toolbox talk should be all about proactive positive attitudes towards health and safety on site.

Engage and involve

Make sure you give your audience plenty of eye contact throughout the talk, and that you are speaking loud enough to be heard by everyone. If people can't hear you or don't feel engaged, they will switch off before you finish.

Speak then listen

Some of the most important outcomes from your toolbox talk will come from the questions and feedback you receive from your workers. Communication is a two-way process, so make sure you show your workers that you are interested in their questions, thoughts and opinions and that you value their feedback.

Give them plenty of opportunities to speak up and be heard. Try asking for input, such as workers own experiences of the topic, to get the conversation going.

Check everyone understands

Make sure that the workforce has understood the toolbox talk. Don't just ask if they have understood - it is far easier to say yes than no, even if they don't understand fully. Ask questions on the subject area and run through various aspects of the talk again if required.

This goes hand in hand with engaging your team and getting them involved in the talk.

Topic: Bee, Wasp, Hornet, and Yellow Jacket Stings

Between one and two million people in the United State are very allergic to stinging insect venom. Every year 90 to 100 people die from sting reactions. Many more deaths may happen, mistakenly diagnosed as heart attacks or sunstrokes or attributed to other causes. More people die yearly from the effects of insect venom than from spider bites.

Stinging insects can present an occupational health problem, mainly for sensitive workers. Usually, danger occurs when workers disturb nests of stinging insects such as bees, wasps, hornets, or yellow jackets.

Mild Reactions

Most people have a mild reaction to bee, wasp, hornet, or yellow jacket stings:

- • Itch
- • Irritation
- • Redness
- • Swelling

For a mild reaction, you can relieve symptoms with ice, baking soda, meat tenderizer, 1% to 2.5% ammonia solution, topical steroids, or oral steroids.

Anaphylaxis

The most severe allergic reactions to stings can be fatal. These reactions, called anaphylaxis, can include life-threatening symptoms:

- • Breathing problems
- • Swelling of the lips or throat
- • Faintness
- • Confusion
- • Rapid heartbeat
- • Hives

For any severe allergic reaction, seek emergency medical help **immediately**. Reaction may occur in a few minutes; death often occurs within 30 minutes.

Preventing Stings

Workers can take some simple steps to prevent stings, both in the open outdoors and in greenhouses.

• Use a commercially available stinging insect control aerosol to destroy nests. It can shoot a high-volume spray stream 15 to 20 feet.

• Do not stand directly under an overhead nest you are trying to destroy. If possible, hire a professional exterminator to remove a nest.

• Never try to burn or flood a nest with water since this will only make stinging insects angry.

• Be careful not to mow over a nest in the ground or disturb a nest in a tree or the eaves of the home.

• Never strike or swing at a wasp or a bee.

• Never trap a wasp or a bee against your body. That can cause the insect to sting.

• Wear a hat and closed shoes (not sandals).

• Light-colored cotton clothing is best. Avoid white or bright-colored, loose-fitting clothing.

• Never wear wool around stinging insects because wool retains some degree of animal odor even after extensive processing.

• Avoid heavy, flowery perfumes, colognes, or scents. They may attract bees.

• Run away from bees, wasps, hornets, or yellow jackets. They are not very fast, and you can usually outrun them.

• Avoid sweet beverages, which can attract stinging insects.

• Do not drink out of a can. Bees might be inside the can where you cannot see them.

Review These Important Points

- Be careful not to mow over a nest in the ground nor disturb a nest in a tree or the eaves of the home.
- The most severe allergic reactions to stings can be life threatening.
- Avoid disturbing nest of bees, wasps, hornets, or yellow jackets.

Topic:		
Instructor:	Location:	
Printed Name	**Signature**	**Date**

Topic: Bucket Truck and Aerial Lifts

According to Occupational Safety and Health Administration (OSHA) statistics, some 30 workers die each year from using aerial lifts. More than half of those involve bucket trucks. Most of the others involve aerial lifts. A tree can strike the bucket and throw the worker out. Power lines might touch the bucket or lift and electrocute the worker.

For more details on related safe practices, refer to these Tailgate Safety Training modules:
- *Preventing Falls From Trees*
- *Overhead Electrical Hazards*
- *Struck-By Accidents*
- *Tree Pruning, Trimming, and Felling Safety*

Bucket Trucks and Aerial Lift Hazards
- Tip-overs
- Falls
- Electrocution
- Being caught between the lift buckets or guardrail and trees
- Being struck by falling branches or trees

General Safety Tips
- Do not operate a lift unless you have receive proper training.
- Keep the lift controls clean and legible.
- Wear a full-body harness when using the bucket truck.
- Always close lift platform chains or doors.
- Stand on the floor of the bucket or lift platform. Do not climb on or lean over guardrails.
- Do not ride on bumpers.
- Do not exceed manufacturer's load-capacity limits.
- Use work-zone warnings like cones and signs if working near traffic.
- Do not modify an aerial lift without written permission of the manufacturer.
- Use proper personal fall protection.

To Prevent Electrocution
- Keep yourself and all objects at least 10 feet away from any conductors.
- Non-electrical workers must stay at least 10 feet away from overhead power lines.
- Electrical workers must insulate power lines. Use proper personal protection tools.
- Insulated buckets help protect against electrocution. However, you must make sure there is no other path for the electricity to ground. **Never** touch another wire.

To Prevent Tip-Overs
- Do not drive with the lift platform elevated.
- Do not exceed vertical or horizontal reach limits.
- Do not exceed the specified load-capacity of the lift.
- On an elevated scissor lift, avoid pushing or pulling.

Review These Important Points
- Always close lift platform chains or doors.
- Do not climb on or lean over guardrails, or ride on bumpers.
- Do not exceed load-capacity limits.

Topic:		
Instructor:	Location:	
Printed Name	**Signature**	**Date**

Topic: Caught In or Between Objects

Green industry workplaces are full of heavy objects that can move — vehicles, equipment, machinery. Many of those objects also have moving parts. Objects that are raised off the ground can fall. When one of those objects moves unexpectedly or falls, it can land on a worker. The worker can be caught between the object and the ground or another object.

Or a worker can be caught in moving machinery parts. Caught-in or caught-between accidents can occur between a power-take-off (PTO) and the shielding, as shown here. Other hazards include pinch points, cut points, and crush points.

Reasons Caught-In and Caught-Between Accidents Happen

• Working on moving equipment.
• Working under mental or physical stress.
• Using unsafe equipment.
• Lack of training or instructions.
• Inadequate guarding on machines.
• Incorrect hitching practices.
• Distraction.

Here are some typical accidents, along with safe practices that could prevent them.

Accident Safety Practice

• While hauling sod, a worker stopped to change a flat truck tire. The truck fell off the jack, pinning the worker between the ground and the truck.
• Two workers were working on a stationary conveyor when it fell off its stands. The workers were caught under the equipment. Never work under a vehicle or equipment that is supported only by a jack or a stand. The jack or stand could tip, and the raised equipment then will be dropped on the person under it.
• A worker removed the shields on the PTO for repairs but failed to replace them after service. Another worker got caught in the PTO. After servicing, all PTO shields **must** be replaced. Only snug-fitting clothing should be worn when working around a PTO. This will prevent clothing from being caught in the PTO.
• A nursery worker unhitched a wagon without chocking the wheels and was run over when the wagon rolled forward.
• A worker forgot to chock the equipment trailer when unloading a mower and was caught between the trailer and the building. While unloading or working on equipment, the wheels of equipment need to be pinned to hold them stationary. This procedure is called chocking. By chocking the wheels, the equipment will be unable to roll and cause injury.
• While backing a loaded equipment trailer to a truck, a worker was caught between the truck and the trailer. When helping someone to hitch equipment or an implement to a truck or tractor, stand to the side. That way, the driver can see you. Also, you won't be between the truck and the equipment.

Review These Important Points

• Always chock a vehicle before doing any work on it.
• Always chock towed equipment before unhitching it.
• Use caution when working with moving equipment.
• Replace shields immediately after service or repairs.
• Never work on raised equipment on a stand — always block it first.

Topic:		
Instructor:	Location:	

Printed Name	Signature	Date

Topic: Chain Saw Safety

Chain saws are great tools for landscapers and arborists. Their powerful motors cut through heavy trunks, branches, and brush quickly and easily. However, that power also brings danger. Safe practices are critical in using chain saws.

Operator's Manual

Keep the operator's manual with the chain saw. A good place to store it is in the chain saw case. If the manual is missing, contact the manufacturer for a replacement. Periodically review the manual for safe operating procedures.

Personal Protection Equipment

Use the proper Personal Protection Equipment (PPE) for the job. Use the following as a guide:
• Clothing should fit well and be free of dangling or ragged edges that can become tangled in the saw.
• Nylon mesh protective leg chaps and/or kneepads can provide increased protection for the legs.
• A hard hat protects the head from falling limbs or branches. A properly fitted hat is cool, comfortable, and provides protection from head injury.
• A full-face shield or safety goggles/glasses that have side shields prevent injury from flying wood chips, twigs, and sawdust.
• Protect ears from the high level of noise by using earplugs in combination with earmuffs.
• Safety boots or shoes with high tops protect ankles in the event of accidental contact with a moving saw blade. Steel-toed boots will help protect the feet from falling limbs or logs.
• Lightweight leather gloves protect hands from cuts, splinters, and abrasions.

Preventive Maintenance

Keep the saw in good repair. Consult the operator's manual and check for needed maintenance before each use. The operator's manual can be the best source of information for this procedure.

When to Sharpen the Saw

• If the chain tends to "walk" sideways while cutting.
• If the cut shows fine powder instead of chips.
• If it is necessary to press hard to cut.
• If you smell burnt wood or see smoke coming from the blade area.
With correct chain tension, you get good cutting action and a long chain life. If too loose, a chain will derail; if too tight, a chain will bind. Proper lubrication prolongs the life of the saw and increases safety.

Follow These Precautions When Fueling and Starting the Chain Saw Engine

• **Never smoke** when you are fueling or using a chain saw.
• With electric saws, use caution to avoid shock hazards.
• Fuel in gasoline-powered saws can cause a fire or burns.
• Only refuel the engine when it is cool.
• Never smoke when working with a power saw.
• To start the saw, always brace the saw by placing it on the ground and putting one foot on the bracket to the rear of the saw.
• Grip the top handle of the saw firmly with one hand and use the other to pull the starting rope.
• **Never** drop-start the saw. That is, never try to start the saw by holding it in one hand while pulling the rope with the other hand.

Transporting and Storing the Chain Saw

Transport a power chain saw in a chain guard or a carrying case. Do not carry the saw in the passenger area of a vehicle. Brace the saw so that it cannot tip.

When storing the saw, drain the fuel tank back into the supply container and run the engine at the idle until it stops. Remove the chain and store in oil. Disconnect the spark plug to prevent an accidental starting. Keep out of the reach of children.

Review These Important Points
• Wear close-fitting clothing.
• Use a face shield or safety goggles, ear protection, safety boots, and gloves.
• Keep equipment in good repair and make adjustments as needed.
• Follow recommendations for refueling and safely starting saws.
• Only use saws that are equipped with chain brakes you can trigger in an emergency or that are automatically triggered by a kickback, a life-threatening situation.

Topic:		
Instructor:	Location:	

Printed Name	Signature	Date

Different chemicals can irritate the skin. Some chemicals remove fats and oils from the skin. When this occurs, the skin becomes cracked and dry. Irritants can also cause severe burns. Or irritants can cause oils and waxes to plug hair follicles and sweat ducts. That can cause dermatitis and acne.

The below table also lists examples and effects.

Dermatitis

With dermatitis, the skin is inflamed and irritated. There are two types:

• **Primary irritation.** Occurs from contact with a chemical irritant.

• **Sensitization.** Skin becomes more sensitive after exposure. Then, just a small amount can cause a severe allergic reaction.

Types and Effects of Chemical Irritants			
Chemical Irritant	**Examples**	**Found In**	**Effects**
Strong acids	Strong acids	Fertilizers Dyes Paint pigments	Severe burns Brief or prolonged effects
	Sulfuric acid	Battery acid Phosphate fertilizers	
	Nitric Acid	Fertilizers Metal working	
Strong caustics	Sodium hydroxide	Soaps, detergents Cleaning products Adhesives Paint remover Disinfectants	
	Potassium hydroxide	Disinfectants Sterilizing agents	
Strong solvents	Dichloromethane N-methylpyrrolidine	Paint remover Alcohol	Prolonged dermatitis Prolonged acne

Chemical Irritant Safety Practices

- Identify hazards before working with chemicals.
- Read the Material Safety Data Sheet (MSDS) and labels on the containers.
- Identify emergency procedures in case an accident occurs.
- Avoid contact with strong chemical irritants.
- Use Personal Protection Equipment.
  - Goggles

- o Gloves
- o Sleeves
- o Aprons
- o Shields
- o Footwear
- In case of exposure
  - o Use showers, eyewash fountains, hand/face spray units, and other emergency equipment.
  - o Call 911 if appropriate.
  - o Report accidental exposures to hazardous substance.

Review These Important Points
• Be aware of all types of skin irritants.
• Know what substances you use that may be dangerous.
• Follow the correct procedures in an emergency.
• Wear protective equipment when on the job.
• Use emergency equipment and call 911 if appropriate.

Topic:		
Instructor:	Location:	
Printed Name	**Signature**	**Date**

Topic: Choosing Spray Nozzles

Nozzles regulate droplet size, spray flow, and spray pattern. The right spray nozzle is critical for safe spraying and effective application. The right nozzle causes less spray drift to unintended areas like other crops or backyards. Other safe techniques can also help reduce spray drift.

Flow regulation affects the application rate. Nozzle opening size and spray pressure affect the flow rate through nozzles. These factors can be varied by selecting a different nozzle size or adjusting the pressure.

Droplet size varies with several factors:

- Pressure
- Weather conditions
  - Temperature
  - Humidity
  - Wind speed and direction
- Nozzle size
- Spray angle
- Spray pattern shape

Usually, increasing nozzle pressure decreases droplet size. Increasing tip spray angle can also decrease droplet size. As shown in the figure, smaller droplets drift longer distances.

Weather has a strong influence on spray drift. Wind direction and speed can cause spray to drift away from its target. The larger the droplet, the faster it falls toward its target, and the less likely it is to drift. However, high winds can cause large droplets to drift off target.

Nozzle Spray Patterns

There are three basic nozzle spray patterns. Each is best for certain applications.

- Flat-spray, or flat-fan, nozzles spray droplets from a flat-spray tip. They form a fan-shaped pattern as they leave the nozzle opening.
  - A flat-spray nozzle is the only kind that puts out herbicide accurately and uniformly.
  - The edges of the pattern have a lower spray volume. So, patterns of adjacent nozzles must overlap to obtain uniform coverage.
  - Wider-angle nozzles produce smaller droplets.
  - Narrow-angle spray tips produce a more penetrating spray. They are also less likely to become clogged.
- Hollow-cone nozzles produce a spray pattern with the liquid on the outside of a cone.
  - These are best when penetration and coverage are critical.
  - The typical spray distribution is saddle-shaped. There is less liquid in the center of the distribution, tapering off rapidly at the edges.
  - It is not well suited for broadcast applications; proper overlap is difficult.
  - Generally produces the smallest droplets.
  - Spray drift can be high because of the many small droplets produced at the normal operating pressure of 40 pounds per square inch (psi) and above.
- Wide-angle full-cone nozzles produce large droplets distributed throughout a full cone.
  - These are good for soil-applied and systemic herbicides.
  - Maximum drift control at pressures of 15 to 20 psi is achieved.
  - The uniform spray pattern is maintained over a pressure range of 10 to 40 pounds per square inch(psi).
  - Droplets are larger than with other tip styles of equal capacity at similar pressures.

Cleaning Nozzles

• Use water that looks clean enough to drink when cleaning the sprayer. Foreign materials in the water can wear out nozzles.

• Watch the output pattern of nozzles periodically. Streaks in the pattern indicate foreign material inside the nozzles.
• Remove and clean nozzles. Use a soft brush for the tip and screen with strong detergent solution or kerosene.
• Use a wooden toothpick to unclog nozzle tips. A pin, a knife, or any other metal object can completely change the spray pattern capacity of the tip.

Spraying Tips to Reduce Drift

• Follow label recommendations to avoid drift with highly volatile pesticides.
• Use nozzles that produce coarser droplets on targets that do not require small, uniformly distributed droplets.
• Keep spray volume up.
• Use nozzles with larger orifices.
• Use nozzles with narrower spray-fan angles.
• Avoid spraying on extremely hot and dry days.
• Do not spray when wind speeds are higher than 5 miles per hour.
• Avoid spraying near sensitive crops downwind. Leave a buffer strip of 50 to 100 feet, and spray the strip later when the wind shifts.

Personal Protection Equipment

Workers must wear proper Personal Protection Equipment (PPE) when working with any type of pesticide, herbicide, or spray. Consult the product label for equipment requirements, such as latex gloves.

Review These Important Points

- Nozzles regulate spray flow, droplet size, and spray pattern.
- Opening size and spray pressure affect flow rate through the nozzle.
- Droplet size varies due to pressure, climatic conditions, and nozzle size.
- There are three basic spray pattern shapes — flat-spray, hollow-cone, and full-cone.

Topic:		
Instructor:	Location:	
Printed Name	**Signature**	**Date**

Topic: Hydration

Water is one of the most important substances on Earth. All plants, animals, and people need water to survive. Water serves very important purposes to our bodies and our bodily functions- some of which you may not even be aware of.

Interesting Facts Regarding Water's Role to Our Bodies

- Water comprises more than 60% of our body weight.
- Lack of water is the #1 trigger for daytime fatigue.
- A 2% drop in water level of the body can spur problems with short term memory.
- Water naturally cleanses the body of toxins.
- Water regulates the body's cooling system.
- Water acts as a lubricant and cushion to our joints.

Hydration Tips

- It is recommended to drink at least 50oz to 64oz of water a day depending on what source you refer to. That is about three to four regular sized water bottles a day. This amount is a minimum amount to shoot for; you may need even more water than that. Many people do not realize how little water they actually drink. Pay attention to how much you drink today and add to it if needed.
- Do not wait until you are thirsty to drink water. By time the body tells you that you are thirsty dehydration is already occurring.
- Other beverages such as soda or coffee steal water from your body and make you more dehydrated. Limit these types of drinks throughout the day.
- Your urine can serve as an indicator whether you are hydrated or not. If your urine is clear or pale and you are using the restroom regularly, you are probably hydrated. If your urine is dark and you are visiting the restroom less frequently, you need to drink more water. While you should not solely rely on this indicator, it can be helpful in gauging whether or not you need to drink more water.

Discussion point:

-How many people think they drink at least 3 to 4 water bottles worth of water a day?

Topic:		
Instructor:	Location:	

Printed Name	Signature	Date

Topic: Slip, Trip, & Fall Basics

Slips, trips and falls is the number 1 reason for a workplace injury in the United States. More workers are hurt due to slips, trip or falls than any other reason. Over the years we've had several incidents from tripping on rugs to slipping on water. This week we'll look specifically at Slips, Trips and Falls.

Thousands of disabling injuries—and even deaths—occur each year as a result of slips, trips, and falls:

- From heights, on stairs, and on level ground
- At work and at home

Maintain Work Areas to Prevent Slips, Trips, and Falls

This is probably the most important thing you can do to prevent this type of accident. Housekeeping is the key to preventing slips, trips and falls.

- Keep walkways, aisles, and stairs free of tools, materials, and other hazards.
- Clean up any leaks or spills on floors, stairs, entranceways, and loading docks promptly.
- Repair or report floor problems, such as broken planks, missing tiles, etc.
- Block off and mark floor areas that are being cleaned or repaired.
- Keep cords, power cables, and air hoses out of walkways.
- Place trash promptly in proper containers.
- Keep drawers closed. Take Precautions on Stairs and Dock Edges
- Report missing or broken stair rails and slippery or damaged treads.
- Walk, don't run, on stairs. Hold onto stair rails while going up and down.
- Don't jump on or off platforms and loading docks, and stay away from edges.
- Don't carry a load you can't see over, especially on stairs or around dock edges.

Topic:		
Instructor:	Location:	

Printed Name	Signature	Date

Topic: Dust and Mold

Landscaping and horticultural work often involve peat, vermiculite, perlite, and mulch. Other organic substances may be frequent, too. Those organic substances produce dust when handled. Molds often grow naturally in the substances, too. Mold spores attach themselves to airborne dust particles.

All workers can be exposed to organic dust and mold. Greenhouse and nursery workers often get heavy exposure. Inhaling moldy dust from peat, vermiculite, perlite, mulch, or other substances can cause different diseases.

Farmer's Lung

Farmer's Lung is a noninfectious allergic disease. Basically, an individual becomes allergic to dust and mold. With Farmer's Lung, the immune system cannot adjust to the mold spores. Farmer's Lung has these symptoms:

- Fatigue
- Chills
- Shortness of breath
- Tightness in the chest
- Headache
- Irritating cough
- Loss of appetite

Respiratory symptoms vary with the amount and intensity of exposure. After a first reaction, a worker is likely to develop an increased sensitivity. Then, a worker can have a more severe reaction with fewer exposures. In Chronic Farmer's Lung, the reaction continues even after all the irritant is gone. It is possible to develop Chronic Farmer's Lung after one acute attack. However, it usually develops slowly over time after repeated exposure. Contact a doctor if concerns about permanent lung damage arise.

Organic Toxic Dust Syndrome

Organic Dust Toxic Syndrome has similar symptoms but does not involve the immune system. Organic Toxic Dust Syndrome goes away after it runs its course. It often hits all the workers in a group at one time.

Bronchitis and Asthma

Exposure to organic dust and mold can cause bronchitis and asthma. Exposure can also aggravate existing bronchitis and asthma.

Using Respirators or Dust Masks

When using respiratory protection, select the appropriate Personal Protection Equipment for the task. A dust mask provides some protection if it is fresh, clean, and fit-tested. However, the best protection is a particulate respirator:

- Tested and certified by the National Institute for Occupational Safety and Health (NIOSH).
- With a Type 95, Type 97, Type 100, or HEPA filter.
- Fit-tested to ensure a tight seal between the facepiece and your face.

Reducing Exposure to Dust and Mold

- Identify dust and mold in the work site. Heavy concentrations of mold spores appear as dry white or gray powder or clouds.
- Minimize the amount and type of dust and mold in your work site.
- Avoid exposure to dust from decayed plants, leaves, mulch, and other materials.
- Limit exposure to all dust and mold.
- Work in a controlled site whenever possible.

- Use mechanical controls to remove dust and mold from the air, where feasible.
- Ventilate dusty areas.
- Move work outside whenever possible.
- Plan outside work to minimize dust exposure. Take natural factors into consideration:
    o Wind direction
    o Windy times of the day
    o Using the dewpoint to settle the dust
- Avoid dusty work in confined areas.

Review These Important Points
- Wear a particulate respirator or dust mask when working with moldy mulches.
- Fit-test particulate respirators and dust masks.
- Work in a well-ventilated area.
- Use exhaust fans when possible to control exposure.
- Seek medical advice when concerned about exposure.
- Know the warning signs of Farmer's Lung.
- Change ventilation filters on a regular schedule.

Topic:		
Instructor:	Location:	

Printed Name	Signature	Date

Topic: Equipment and Plant Transport

Many landscaping and horticultural businesses use trucks and trailers to transport equipment and plants to work sites. Types of equipment can include lawn mowers, both push type and riding type; small backhoes; tractors, etc. You should know safe procedures to:

- Secure equipment on a truck bed or trailer.
- Perform a safety check before driving.
- Drive while towing a trailer.
- Secure plants or small trees for delivery to a work site in a truck bed or a trailer.

Securing Equipment for Safe Transport

- While loading or unloading a truck or trailer, be sure that the parking brake is set and that the wheels are chocked. This will keep the truck or trailer from accidentally moving while it is being loaded or unloaded.
- Always make sure the load is properly balanced. An unbalanced load can cause a trailer to sway and be hard to control. An unbalanced load could cause a traffic accident.
- Only use a truck or trailer that has side rails.
- Use chains or straps with ratchet load binders to secure the equipment to the bed. A chain or strap with a ratchet type binder will ensure that the equipment is securely anchored to the bed.
- Always make sure that gasoline cans are secure and not loose in the bed.
- Secure tools such as rakes, shovels, hoes, picks, ladders, etc., with tie down straps or bungee cords. Never leave these tools unsecured in the bed or trailer.

Securing Plants for Safe Transport

- While loading or unloading a truck or trailer, be sure that the parking brake is set and that the wheels are chocked. This will keep the truck or trailer from accidentally moving while it is being loaded or unloaded.
- Always make sure the load is properly balanced. An unbalanced load can cause a trailer to sway and be hard to control. That could cause a traffic accident.
- Plants can be heavy, so use proper lifting techniques.
- Only use a truck or trailer that has side rails.
- Use tie down straps or bungee cords to secure plant pallets or flats to the bed of the truck or trailer. This will reduce the chance of the load shifting.
- If necessary, attach a cargo net over the load.
- If small trees or tree saplings are being transported, secure them in an upright position using tie-down straps or bungee cords.

Trailer Towing Safety Tips: Before You Start

- Make sure that the weight of the equipment being loaded does not exceed the Gross Combination Weight Rating. This information should be stated on the trailer itself or in the operator's manual. If you are not sure, ask your employer.
- Use the proper hitch.
- Check the hitch and the ball to make sure they are properly secured. Make sure the safety chains are in place. Lock the hitch with a padlock and bar.
- Check tail lights, running lights, directional signals, and brake lights. Replace any burned out bulbs before towing the trailer.
- If the trailer has its own braking system, check the braking system before towing.
- Check the truck mirrors so that you have good side and rear visibility.
- Check the tire pressure and tread wear on the truck and trailer tires.

- Make sure the load is properly secured and balanced.
- After the safety check, report any problems to your employer.

Trailer Towing Safety Tips: On the Road
- Avoid jerky starts or fast acceleration. This can cause the load to shift.
- While driving, avoid sharp turns. Normal turns should be wider to prevent jackknifing or curb jumping.
- Never exceed the speed limit when towing a trailer.
- Always use turn signals when changing lanes and allow plenty of distance when changing lanes.
- Always come to a stop gradually. Avoid sudden stops.
- Be aware of crosswinds. Crosswinds can cause the trailer to drift into another lane.
- Be alert when you are passed by large trucks or semi trucks. The wind they produce can cause the trailer to sway. As they pass, reduce your speed gradually. Do not speed up. steer straight ahead.
- Occasionally check the position of the trailer using the truck mirrors.
- Remember that a loaded trailer handles differently than an empty trailer.
- Always have proper identification while operating a company vehicle.
- Once you have reached the work site and have stopped, set the parking brake and chock the trailer wheels before unloading.
- If you have to back the trailer, use opposite steering procedures. It is a good idea to practice backing a trailer. Always back slowly. Sharp turns can result in the trailer jackknifing. If necessary, have another worker outside the truck help you back the trailer by using hand signals.

Review These Important Points
- Always set the parking brake and chock the wheels before loading or unloading a trailer.
- Always make sure the load is properly balanced and secured.
- Secure all small tools with bungee cords or tie down straps.
- Use proper lifting techniques when manually loading and unloading.
- Do a safety check before towing a trailer.
- Obey all traffic laws while towing a trailer.
- Drive slowly while backing a trailer. Avoid sharp turns.

Topic:		
Instructor:	Location:	
Printed Name	**Signature**	**Date**

Topic: Equipment with Cutter Bars and Blades

Equipment with cutter bars or blades includes sickle cutter bars, rotary disk cutting blades, and hand-held powered cutting devices. When using cutting equipment, the operator should be familiar with the mechanisms and safety precautions.

Working with Cutter Bars and Blades

- Keep hands and feet away from the cutter bar or blade when the machine is running. Shut off the power before unclogging, servicing, or moving the machine.
- Mowers with rotating disks can throw objects. Do not operate when bystanders are near. Thrown objects can cause serious injury.
- Use the mower safety curtain or cover when operating the cutter bar or blades. Safety curtains prevent objects from being thrown by the rotating disks.
- Safety curtains may not catch all flying objects. Use personal eye protection to prevent injury from anything thrown — personal eye protection, protective gloves, and hard hats.
- Tractors with cabs offer additional protection from thrown objects.
- Keep knives and fastening hardware in good condition. This prevents knives from being thrown from the machine. Consult the operator's manual for directions.

Follow These Steps to Safely Unclog the Cutter Bar or Blade and Remove Debris

- Stop and disengage the power-take-off (PTO) or drive clutch.
- Raise the cutting and mowing device and back up.
- Move the machine clear of the accumulated debris.
- Shut off the engine. With the parking brake engaged, shift the transmission into park or neutral.
- Pull the clogged debris away from the cutter bar or blade.
- Check the cutter bar or blade for broken or damaged parts.
- Return the safety curtain or cover to the proper operating position.
- Start the engine. Engage the PTO at low speed. Then increase it to the rated speed.

Knives and rotating disks on cutter bars and blades can cause severe injury if used improperly. Rocks or other debris thrown by rotating disks, blades, and knives can injure the operator or bystanders. Follow all safety precautions.

Review These Important Points

- Always disengage the PTO before attempting to service any cutting device.
- Use and maintain all machine shields and covers.
- Use personal eye protection as added protection.
- When pulling debris out of cutter bars or blades, pull away from the knives.

Topic:		
Instructor:	Location:	
Printed Name	**Signature**	**Date**

Topic: First Aid Kit

Knowing how and what types of first aid to use can prevent a more serious injury. Keep a Red Cross First Aid manual with the first-aid kit.

The Red Cross suggests that the kit include:
- Poison first-aid kit with syrup of Ipecac and charcoal
- Sterile first-aid dressings in sealed envelopes (2" x 2" for small wounds, 4" x 4" for larger wounds and for a compress to stop bleeding)
- Tongue blades
- Bandage scissors
- Tweezers
- Eye wash solution
- Thermometer
- Safety pins
- Ace bandage
- Band-aids
- Roller bandage, 1" x 5 yards (for finger)
- Roller bandage, 2" x 5 yards (to hold dressings in place)
- Adhesive tape
- Triangular bandages for a sling or as a covering over a larger dressing
- Cotton balls for cleaning wounds or applying medication
- Splints 1/4" thick, 1/2" wide, and 12 to 15" long for splinting broken arms and legs
- 70 percent isopropyl alcohol and tincture of green soap in a covered container for cleaning
- Ice packs (chemical ice bags) to use to reduce swelling
- Insect bite kit
- Several pairs of disposable gloves
- Waterless hand wash

There are many types of first-aid kits available. Keep and maintain an appropriate kit on each major piece of equipment, trucks, and cars and in the garage or shop. Kits should be inspected at least twice a month and replenished as necessary.

The Red Cross suggests that workers be certified in emergency cardiopulmonary resuscitation (CPR), the method used to restore heartbeat and breathing. CPR may save the life of someone who has been injured or suffers a serious illness. However, CPR and first aid take training. An untrained individual who gives CPR or first aid may cause harm.

Having an emergency plan in place saves time during an accident. Have a plan for every work location, including machinery sheds, garage, greenhouses, and fields. Know and practice what to do in case of an emergency.

If a Serious Accident Occurs
- Stay calm and try to calm the victim.
- Shout or radio for help and tell a specific person to call 911 for Emergency Medical Service (EMS).
- Evaluate the victim's condition and administer first aid or CPR as needed. (Only trained individuals should administer CPR first aid). Continue treatment until relieved by the EMS personnel.
- Do not move the victim except to protect the victim from further injury.
- Remain with the victim.
- Conduct a quick rescue without risking personal safety.

When calling 911, give the dispatcher the information listed here and remain on the phone until the information is confirmed and the dispatcher says to hang up:

- Location of and directions to the emergency
- Type of emergency
- Number of victims
- Location phone number
- Treatment given to the victim(s)

Review These Important Points

- Have a complete first aid kit on all major implements and in all work locations.
- Learn first aid and CPR.
- Know the emergency medical plan and keep it current.
- Know the 911 number and accident information.

Topic:		
Instructor:	Location:	

Printed Name	Signature	Date

Topic: Lightning Safety

Lightning is a dangerous natural force. Approximately 300 people a year are struck by lightning averaging 50 deaths a year in the last 30 years.

Employers, supervisors, and workers should understand lightning risks, and precautions to minimize workplace hazards. Lightning is unpredictable and can strike up to 10 miles from any rainfall. Many lightning victims are caught outside during a storm because they did not act promptly to get to a safe place, or they go back outside too soon after a storm has passed. Proper planning and safe practices can easily increase lightning safety when working outdoors.

Planning for lightning on the construction site:
- Identify the safe shelter areas.
- Check a weather app before the start of the workday.
- Review the company lightning policy and procedures.
- Have an emergency plan in place for your work site.
- Know where the nearest medical treatment center is located.

Lightning: What You Need to Know
- NO PLACE outside is safe when thunderstorms are in the area!!
- If you hear thunder, lightning is close enough to strike you.
- When you hear thunder, immediately move to safe shelter: a substantial building with electricity or plumbing or an enclosed, metal-topped vehicle with windows up.
- Stay in safe shelter at least 30 minutes after you hear the last sound of thunder.

Indoor Lightning Safety
- Stay off corded phones, computers and other electrical equipment that put you in direct contact with electricity.
- Avoid plumbing, including sinks, baths and faucets.
- Stay away from windows and doors, and stay off porches.
- Do not lie on concrete floors, and do not lean against concrete walls.

Topic:		
Instructor:	Location:	

Printed Name	Signature	Date

Topic: Forklift Safety

A forklift or powered industrial truck can be dangerous if operated by untrained workers. The driver or bystanders can be seriously injured or killed if an accident should occur. Forklifts can also cause damage to the employer's property. Good safety procedures for operating a forklift should be followed at all times.

Safety: Before Operating

- Do not operate a forklift if you have not been properly trained in all operations and safety procedures.
- Never operate a forklift without permission from a supervisor.
- Check brakes, steering, controls, forks, hoist, fire extinguisher, warning devices, and lights at the beginning and end of each shift. Do not operate a forklift if any item on the checklist fails inspection. Report all problems to your supervisor.
- Pay attention to maximum load limits. Never overload.
- All forklifts should be equipped with a multi-purpose dry chemical fire extinguisher.

Safety: During Transport

- **No riders on forklifts!**
- Make sure the load is balanced before and during transport.
- Check the ground or floor for uneven areas and debris.
- Always travel at a safe speed.
- Tilt the forklift masts back when driving the forklift. This will lessen the chance of the load becoming unbalanced.
- Never reach through the mast for any reason. If a load has shifted, stop the forklift, lower the forks, put the forklift into park, and set the brake. If necessary, have another worker help you reposition the load.
- Keep the forks about 4 to 6 inches above the ground when moving a load.
- If you cannot see because of the size of the load, drive in reverse slowly. If necessary, have another worker guide you and serve as a lookout.
- Use standard hand signals for communication.
- Do not speed. The forklift should be driven at about 5 miles per hour. This speed is the same as a normal walk.
- Watch out for other forklifts and workers.
- Always back the forklift down a ramp. Keep the load in front when going uphill.
- Always keep your head, arms, and legs inside the driving compartment.
- Operators should always wear hard hats in high lift areas.
- Never lift people.
- Never lift a load above workers. Never allow workers to stand under a raised load.
- Sound the horn when approaching a corner.
- Remember that when you turn a corner, the rear of the forklift makes a wide swing. Watch for clearance on both sides of the aisle.
- Check side and overhead clearances when loading and unloading.
- Watch for water, oil, or other liquids on the floor. Report any wet surface to your supervisor.
- Watch out for overhead hazards such as pipes, beams, lights, sprinklers, door casings, cable wires, and signs.
- Always be careful around loading docks. Do not operate the forklift too close to the edge of the dock. Many forklift accidents occur when a forklift backs off a dock.

- Do not turn the wheels too fast. This can cause the forklift to overturn.

Safety: Stacking Materials

- Always stack materials so they are tied in. For example, if you have six loads to stack, put three on the floor, two on the second tier, and one on the top. This forms a pyramid and lessens the possibility of materials falling.
- Do not stack materials too high. This can cause materials to fall.
- Make sure that stacked materials do not block the building's sprinkler system.

Review These Important Points

- All employees need to be properly trained before operating a forklift.
- Do a forklift safety check before and after each shift.
- Do not overload the forklift.
- Check all clearances while operating a forklift.
- Watch out for other forklifts and workers while operating a forklift.
- Never allow anyone to ride on the forklift.
- Use caution when turning corners.
- Never speed while operating a forklift.
- Always be alert around loading docks.

Topic:		
Instructor:	Location:	
Printed Name	**Signature**	**Date**

Topic: Distracted Driving – Cellphone Use

Using cellphones or other devices while driving has proven to be deadly. Cellphone use during driving is very prevalent on our roads today. In fact, at any given time throughout the day, approximately 660,000 drivers are attempting to use their phones while behind the wheel of an automobile.

Smartphones have made it easy for us to stay connected at all times. But that can pose serious safety risks if someone decides to check his or her text messages, emails, phone calls, or any other mobile applications while driving.

Some Statistics about Cellphone Use and Driving:

- The National Safety Council reports that cell phone use while driving leads to 1.6 million crashes each year.
- In 2013, 3,154 people were killed in distraction-related crashes.
- Nearly 330,000 injuries occur each year from accidents caused by texting while driving.
- 1 out of every 4 car accidents in the United States is caused by texting and driving.
- Texting while driving is 6x more likely to cause an accident than driving drunk.
- Answering a text takes away your attention for about five seconds. Traveling at 55 mph, that's enough time to travel the length of a football field.
- Texting while driving causes a 400% increase in time spent with eyes off the road.

Mitigation Actions for Distracted Driving:

- Put the cell phone down while driving.
- Put your cellphone on airplane mode if needed to eliminate distractions as well as the urge to answer a text, call, or email alert.
- If you need to text or call while driving pull over to a safe area to do so.
- When traveling as a passenger, urge any driver who is using their cellphone to put it down.
- If there is another driver on the road who is using a phone while driving, maintain a safe distance from them and be a defensive driver. Always leave yourself an out in case of any type of accident occurs around your vehicle.

Discussion points:

1. Has distracted driving impacted anyone you know?
2. *Discuss your company's cell phone/electronics use policy on the job.*

Topic:		
Instructor:		Location:

Printed Name	Signature	Date

Topic: Heat Stress

Controlling heat stress is very important to pesticide workers and early entry workers. Early entry workers go into an area while entry is restricted after pesticide treatment and must wear protective gear. However, heat stress can affect anyone!

Heat stress is a buildup of body heat caused either internally by muscle use or externally by the environment. Sometimes, the body is overwhelmed by heat. If so, heat exhaustion and heat stroke result. As the heat increases, body temperature and the heart rate rise painlessly. An increase in body temperature of two degrees Fahrenheit can affect mental functioning. A five degree Fahrenheit increase can result in serious illness or death. During hot weather, heat illness may be an underlying cause of other types of injuries, such as heart attacks, falls, and equipment accidents.

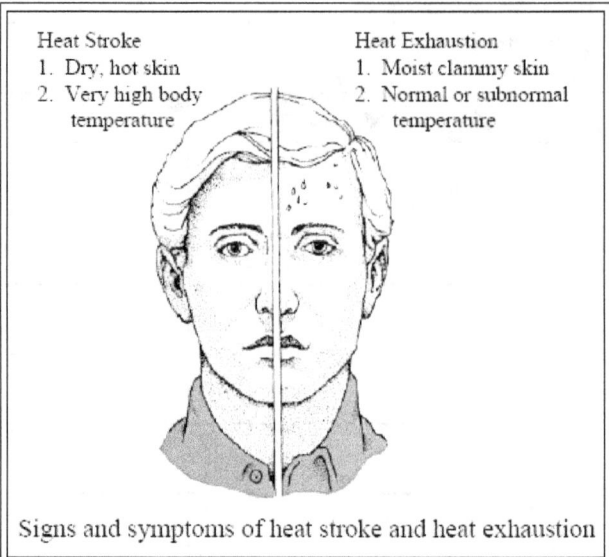

Heat Stroke
1. Dry, hot skin
2. Very high body temperature

Heat Exhaustion
1. Moist clammy skin
2. Normal or subnormal temperature

Signs and symptoms of heat stroke and heat exhaustion

The most serious heat-related illness is heat stroke. The symptoms are confusion, irrational behavior, convulsions, coma, and death. More than 20 percent of heat stroke victims die regardless of health or age. Younger workers seem to be more susceptible to heat stroke than adults. One side effect of heat stroke is heat sensitivity. In other words, once you have had a heat stroke, you are more sensitive to high temperatures for the rest of your life. Varying degrees of brain and kidney damage can also occur.

Preventing Heat Stress Will

• **Protect health** — Heat illness is preventable and treatable before it is life threatening.
• **Improve safety** — Any heat stress can impair functioning.
• **Increase productivity** — People work slower and less
Efficiently when they are suffering from heat stress.
Everyone has an essential role to play in preventing heat stress.
Each member of the team should use good judgment to prevent heat-related illness. A heat stress control program should protect all workers.
These workers range from those who can work comfortably in heat to those in poor physical shape.

To Control Heat Stress

- When possible, schedule heavy tasks and work requiring protective gear for cooler morning or evening hours.
- In prolonged, extremely hot temperatures, nonessential tasks should be postponed.
- Drink one glass of water every 15 to 30 minutes, depending on the heat and humidity. This is the best way to replace lost body fluid.
- Read medication labels to know how they cause the body to react to the sun and heat.
- Avoid alcohol and drugs as they can increase the effects of heat.
- Build up tolerance for working in the heat. Heat tolerance is normally built up over a one- to two-week time period.
- Take breaks to cool down. A 10- to 15-minute break every two hours is effective.
- Adapt work and pace to the weather.
- Provide heat stress training to workers and supervisors.
- Manage work activities. Match them to employees' physical condition.

- Use special protective gear, such as cooling garments, headbands, and cooling vests on early entry workers.
- Know heat stress first-aid techniques.

Heat Exhaustion First Aid
- Move the victim to a cool place.
- Keep the victim lying down with legs straight and elevated 8 to 12 inches.
- Cool the victim by applying cold packs or wet towels or cloths. Fan the victim.
- Give the victim cold water if he or she is fully conscious.
- If no improvement is noted within 30 minutes, seek medical attention.

Heat Stroke First Aid
- Move the victim to a cool place. Monitor temperature. Remove heavy clothing. Light clothing can be left in place.
- Cool the victim right away by any available means, such as placing ice packs at areas with abundant blood supply (neck, armpits, and groin). Wet towels or sheets are also effective. The cloths should be kept wet with cool water.
- To prevent hypothermia, continue cooling the victim until his/her temperature drops to 102° Fahrenheit.
- Keep the victim's head and shoulders slightly elevated.
- Seek medical attention right away. All heat stroke victims need hospitalization.
- Care for seizures if they occur.
- Do not use aspirin or acetaminophen.

Personal Protection Equipment and Heat Stress
Most Personal Protection Equipment (PPE) limits sweat evaporation but not sweat production. Chemicalresistant suits can cause rapid thirst if sweat is not replaced. To slow the buildup of heat when wearing PPE, use special cooling wear.
• **If the temperature is above 70° Fahrenheit** — Cooling vests may be useful when pesticide handlers are wearing chemical-resistant suits. They are either doing heavy or moderate work for a prolonged period.
• **If the temperature is above 80° Fahrenheit** — Working in chemical-resistant suits for more than a half hour without taking frequent water and rest breaks is unsafe. Cooling garments and frequent breaks are recommended.
Breathing resistance is minimized, and the air stream has a cooling effect. Thus, powered air-purifying respirators and supplied-air respirators generally feel cooler than other types of respirators.

Review These Important Points
- Heat stress is serious. Heat stress should be handled as such.
- As strain from heat increases, body temperature and heart rate can rise rapidly.
- Exposure to heat can be serious to workers of all ages.
- Have plenty of liquids available. Administer first aid as needed.

Topic:		
Instructor:	Location:	
Printed Name	**Signature**	**Date**

Topic: Back Injury Prevention

Back injuries are some of the most prevalent and hardest-to-prevent injuries on the job. According to the Bureau of Labor Statistics, more than one million workers suffer back injuries each year, and back injuries account for one of every five workplace injuries or illnesses. These types of injuries account for a large majority of worker's compensation claims every year.

Back injuries often occur when:

- An individual is lifting up an object
- Using improper lifting techniques such as lifting with the back and not the legs
- Lifting an object that is too heavy for the individual
- Twisting while lifting or carrying objects
- Repetitive lifting during a work task

Ways to Prevent Back Injuries

Eliminate– The best way to protect individuals against back injuries is to eliminate as many lifts as possible during the workday. Using equipment such as forklifts, heavy equipment, dollies, etc are the best way to achieve eliminating handling and lifting objects by hand. Break down large or heavy objects that pose a hazard when lifting into smaller safer loads when possible.

Engineering Controls– Setup work areas that are ergonomically friendly to all employees. Install mechanical lifting devices and conveyor belts where feasible to limit handling objects. Install proper shelving and setup storage areas that keep objects and lifts within an optimal range. Keeping objects within the proper range helps keep employees from making awkward or dangerous lifts that can result in a sprain.

Administrative Controls– Use the buddy system when lifting any awkward or heavy objects. Agree on weight limits for lifting. For example, having a policy to not lift anything over 100lbs as a team without first involving a supervisor to see if there is a safer way to complete the lift is an administrative control. Also, always select employees who are physically capable of making the lifts of a task before the work begins.

Personal protective equipment such as back supports or back belts have not shown to be overly effective in preventing back injuries. These devices often create a false sense of security when completing lifts. Individuals should focus on stretching and using proper lifting techniques over using a back belt to keep them safe.

Discussion points:

1. Are there hazardous lifts we can eliminate in our daily operations?
2. Are we using engineering controls when we cannot eliminate a lift or are we just completing the lifts without looking at a safer way to do them?

Topic:		
Instructor:	Location:	
Printed Name	**Signature**	**Date**

Topic: Dealing with Stress from Home

Our home life often overlaps with our work and vice versa, both in good ways and bad ways. Stressors at home can begin to pile up and affect our work if we are not careful. While some stress is so great that the worker experiencing it should not be at work, most stress can be handled in such a way that it does not create a hazardous situation.

Common Stressors Relating to Home Life

There are many different stressors in each of our lives at any given time. It is important to recognize types of common stressors and if they could be affecting you at work. Some common types of stressors include:

- Health. Many people are dealing with health issues, whether it is themselves or a loved one. A serious health scare can be one of the most trying situations we ever deal with in life.
- Finances. Lack of money or excessive bills can weigh heavy on a person.
- Relationships. Fighting or arguing with a loved one can create a stressful situation for an individual long after the discussion was had.
- Fill in the blank. While the above three

mentioned stressors are common for many people, literally anything can be a stressor for an individual. We are all unique and different living different lives; what causes stress for each of us varies greatly.

How Stress Affects Work

There are many negative effects when someone carries in stress from home to work. A couple examples include:

1. Lack of focus. Dealing with any of the above stressors is obviously going to come with a mental load. Constantly giving thought to a stressful situation takes your mind off of the task at hand.
2. Strain on work relationships. Stress can cause a person to shut down or become angry towards those around them. This situation negatively affects communication between workers and the cohesiveness of a work group as a whole. Lack of communication or teamwork can lead to injury.

How to Deal with Stress

There is no one size fits all solution for dealing with stress from a situation at home. Mentioned above, everyone is different and how we each deal with stress will vary. Some quick ideas:

- Recognize what is truly bothering you. From there it is less difficult to attempt to find solutions in dealing with it. Also recognizing the stressor can help you separate your anger towards a situation or person at home from those around you at work.
- Take action to mitigate or eliminate the stressor. Not all stressors can be eliminated, but our reaction and how we face it can be improved.
- Have a conversation with a loved one, friend, or coworker about the issue. Many times our minds are our own worst enemies.
- Have hobbies or other ways to relax. Everyone needs a mental break from work and any stress caused at home.

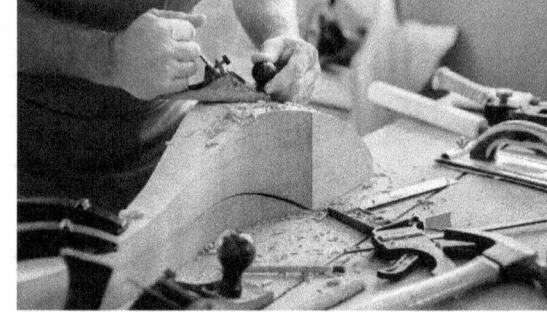

Summary

This was a just a brief discussion on the stressors our home life can cause and how it affects our work. Dealing with the mentioned issues is not easy. However it is important to recognize their existence and how it affects you on a larger scale. If your mind is not in the game at work have a discussion with a supervisor. If needed, take a day off to come into work in a healthier frame of mind.

Topic:		
Instructor:	Location:	
Printed Name	**Signature**	**Date**

Topic: Laundering Pesticide-Contaminated Clothing

Workers should always wear Personal Protection Equipment (PPE) when working with pesticides. However, even with PPE, regular work clothing absorbs pesticides. Your skin can then absorb the pesticides. Clothing can be decontaminated by washing. Pesticide-Contaminated Clothing (PCC) must be washed separately and properly. This also applies to reusable PPE.

Your employer should provide you with clean PPE. You should not take contaminated PPE home for cleaning — it will contaminate your home.

Before Laundering PCC

Read the pesticide label first. It may give directions for the laundering process. All clothing worn while working with pesticides should be considered contaminated. The clothing should be separated from other clothing. Wear rubber gloves when working with PCC. PCC should be washed after each use. It is easier to remove pesticides daily than to remove accumulated contamination. PCC should not be dry cleaned. PCC should not be washed in a public laundromat.

Before laundering PCC, check with local or state agencies for proper disposal of contaminated rinse water. After taking off clothing, use soap and water to wash your hands, face, neck, and forearms. Then take a shower.

Laundering PCC

- Pre-rinse or pre-soak clothing. Pre-soak PCC with similar pesticides together.
- PCC should be washed separately from household laundry.
- The washer should not be overloaded. Wash a few items at a time.
- Use only hot water (140 to 160 degrees).
- The water level should be on the highest setting. Run a full cycle (12 minutes) using a double rinse.
- Dry soap should be used to clean dry forms of pesticides. Liquid detergent should be used to clean liquid forms of pesticides.
- Use 25 percent more soap when clothing has been treated with a soil- or water-repellent finish (i.e., Scotchguard™ or Zepel™).
- Bleach should not be used. It does not remove pesticide residue. It can react with ammonia fertilizer to form chlorine gas. This can be fatal.
- All laundered clothing should be line dried. Sunlight will help break down any pesticide residue left in the clothing. Also, line drying will keep the dryer from becoming contaminated.
- Store PPE clothing in a clean, dry place. Store away from other clothing. Store away from pesticides. Store away from pesticide containers.
- Clean the washing machine by running the empty washer through a full wash cycle with hot water and soap. This is an important step. If the washer is not decontaminated, other clothing will become contaminated.

Pesticides Cannot Be Removed From

- Leather boots
- Leather watchbands
- Inner bands on caps and some decorative items
- Severely contaminated clothing

Warning

- Do not wash limited-use coveralls if they have been contaminated with pesticides.
- Treat contaminated coveralls the same way you would treat the pesticide. Wear gloves and other PPE to protect yourself from pesticide residues within the clothing.

Reusable Coated/Laminated Suits

Suits made from materials such as polyvinyl chloride (PVC) or nitrile should not be decontaminated in a washer. Instead, hose them off. Then wash them in a tub of hot soapy water. Protective clothing made of nitrile, PVC, or other rubber-like compounds should be line dried. However, line dry them in the shade. Sunlight is harmful and will damage the suits. Suits made from plastic, nitrile, or latex may melt if placed in a dryer.

Review These Important Points

- Pesticide-contaminated clothing should be washed separately from other clothing.
- Use the maximum water level and the hottest water. Line dry the clothing.
- Clean the washer with a full wash cycle using hot water.
- Contaminated coveralls should be treated the same way you would treat the pesticide.

Topic:		
Instructor:	Location:	

Printed Name	Signature	Date

Topic: Material Handling Devices

Mechanical devices can be a great help in moving materials, from equipment to containerized plants and bags of mulch. A variety of devices can reduce physical exertion and simplify the job. But those devices also present risks and must be used safely.

Hand Trucks

- Wheelbarrows, dolly trucks, and two-wheeled utility trucks are all referred to as hand trucks.
- Two-wheeled hand trucks can lift and transport heavy, bulky objects short distances.
- Work gloves and safety shoes should be worn. Steel-toe shoes are best.
- Hand trucks should be equipped with canvas, leather, or rubber knuckle guards to help prevent hand injuries.
- Check for defects before loading — loose parts, torn wheels, greasy surfaces. Reports defects you find.
- Use proper lifting techniques when lifting a load.
- When loading, the heavy objects should be below the lighter ones, and the load should be kept as low as possible.
- The load should be balanced over the axles.
- Make sure the load does not hang over the edges.
- The hand truck should not be overloaded, and the load should not obstruct your view.
- The operator should push and balance the truck and should always walk forward.
- If the truck has brakes, use them. Don't hold the truck in place with your foot.

Conveyors

- Generally, conveyors used in industry are roller, belt, screw, bucket, chain, overhead trolley, portable, mobile, tow, or assembly types.
- Moving parts should be guarded with metal or wire mesh enclosures or railings.
- Rollers or pulleys at the ends of belt conveyors should be guarded to prevent fingers and hands from being drawn into pinch points.
- A shield, guard, or housing should enclose each end and all other areas at floor level where workers could come in contact with moving parts.
- Avoid riding on conveyors, except those that incorporate platforms and control rooms for operating personnel.
- Conveyors should have conveniently located warning devices and emergency stop controls.
- Turn off power and lock the switch during maintenance.

Review These Important Points

- All employees should be trained before operating machinery.
- Watch for co-workers when completing work tasks.
- Make sure all loads are balanced when moving.
- Keep all screens and safety shields in place.
- Use standard hand signals for communication.

Topic:		
Instructor:		Location:

Printed Name	Signature	Date

Topic: Mixing and Spraying Pesticides

All workers who mix and spray pesticides must be properly trained to ensure their safety. This training must be conducted within the first five days of employment. The U.S. Environmental Protection Agency (EPA) offers Worker Protection Standard (WPS) training. (Details are available at: www.epa.gov/oppfead1/safety/workers/training.htm.) Training is usually conducted by state agencies. (Details are available at: www.epa.gov/oppfod01/safety/applicators/statepro.htm.)

Employers who have received WPS training can provide this training or hire someone who has been WPS trained. During the training session, you should always ask questions if you do not understand a point of instruction.

WPS training contains requirements for:

- Pesticide safety training
- Notification of pesticide applications
- Use of Personal Protection Equipment (PPE)
  - Gloves
  - Footwear
  - Eye protection
  - Head protection
  - Clothing
  - Respirators
- Restricted entry intervals following pesticide application
- Decontamination supplies
- Emergency medical assistance

Proper Mixing of Pesticides

- Before mixing, test the sprayer with water to see if it leaks and is working properly.
- Read the label to determine the proper mixture.
- Wear PPE while mixing pesticides.
- Mix in a grassy area. Do not mix on concrete or hard surfaces.
- Only use water unless directed by the label to use another liquid.
- Fill the sprayer with two-thirds of the water needed. Then add the proper amount of pesticide. Then add the remaining one-third of water.
- Mix only the amount necessary to do the job.

Proper Spraying of Pesticides

- Spray so that other workers or persons are not exposed.
- Other workers and persons must not enter the area where a pesticide is being sprayed.
- Be aware of wind direction. Wind can cause the pesticide to drift to areas not chosen for spraying.
- If possible, spray early in the morning or in late afternoon. High humidity will lessen the chance of drifting.
- Wear PPE while spraying. Also, PPE must be worn during the restricted, early-entry period.
- All workers must be notified in advance of where spraying is to occur.
- All workers must have immediate access to water, soap, and towels for routine washing and emergency decontamination.
- Anyone exposed to a pesticide must be taken to a medical facility. Tell medical personnel the type of pesticide being used.
- All workers must be informed of pesticide label requirements. Central posting of recent applications is required.

Clean Up and Proper Disposal of Pesticide Containers

- Rinse all equipment with water in a grassy area. Never clean up on a hard surface.
- Never flush pesticide residue into a storm drain or any type of drain.
- Always wash with soap and water before you eat, drink, smoke, or go the bathroom.
- Clothing worn during spraying should be washed separately.
- Before discarding an empty container, fill it half full of water. Shake it to rinse. Empty the rinse water into the sprayer. Spray in a grassy area. Do this three times. This process will also clean the sprayer bottle and hose.
- Once the container has been completely rinsed, punch a hole in the bottom. Wrap the container in newspaper- and place in the trash.
- Do not burn empty containers.
- Do not recycle containers.

Review These Important Points

- All workers must be properly trained in the mixing and spraying process.
- The EPA offers WPS training.
- Read the label to determine the proper mixture.
- PPE must be worn while mixing and spraying.
- Rinse all equipment with water in a grassy area. Never clean up on a hard surface.

Topic:		
Instructor:	Location:	

Printed Name	Signature	Date

Topic: Mosquito Bites

Mosquitoes prey on blood for nutrition. They feed on many different donors every day. They can contract diseases like malaria or West Nile Virus from any one of those donors. When they bite humans, they can pass those diseases to humans in their saliva.

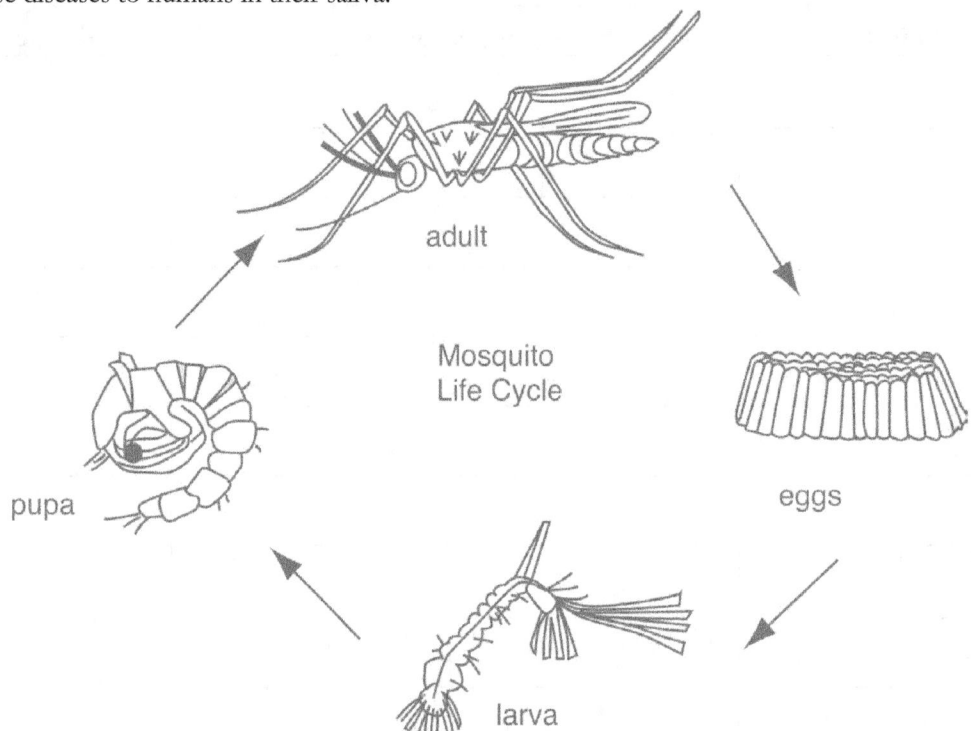

Mosquito bites result in slight allergic reactions — they swell and itch. Too much scratching can lead to bleeding and scabbing. It can cause secondary infection. Take these steps to help control swelling and itching:

- Wash the area with soap and water.
- Put on some calamine lotion or anti-itch cream to help stop the itching
- Place an ice pack on the bite; this will also help stop itching.

West Nile Virus

Mosquitoes can transmit serious diseases such as mosquito-borne encephalitis, malaria, and West Nile Virus. The West Nile Virus originated in Africa. It has now established itself in the United States.

Mosquitoes become infected when they feed on infected animals, especially birds. The mosquitoes can then transmit the virus to humans when they bite humans. During the bite, the virus is injected into the human where it multiplies and may cause disease.

Workers should be on the lookout for symptoms of West Nile Virus in particular. Mild symptoms include:

- Fever
- Headache
- Body aches
- Skin rash
- Swollen lymph glands

Severe symptoms of West Nile Virus include:

- Neck stiffness
- Disorientation
- Stupor

- Coma
- Tremors
- Convulsions
- Muscle weakness
- Convulsions and paralysis

If workers have either mild or severe symptoms, they should seek medical assistance quickly.

Preventing Mosquito Bites

- Stay indoors at dawn and dusk and in the early evening, if possible.
- Wear long pants and long sleeves outdoors.
- Use space sprays or aerosol foggers for rapid knockdown of mosquitoes.
- Apply residual sprays to tall grasses, weeds, trees, shrubs, and outbuildings one to two days before use of the area.

Cautions

- Use water solutions instead of oil-based formulations to prevent plant injury.
- Dead birds such as crows can be tested for West Nile Virus if they have been dead less than 48 hours. To handle dead birds, always use rubber gloves or a shovel.

Review These Important Points

- Mosquitoes can acquire a disease every time they bite an animal or a human.
- Mosquitoes can also transmit a disease every time they bite.
- Residual sprays applied to tall grasses, weeds, trees, shrubs, and outbuildings, one to two days before use of the area, are effective in preventing mosquito bites.

Topic:		
Instructor:	Location:	
Printed Name	**Signature**	**Date**

Topic: Safety Data Sheet

The Safety Data Sheet (SDS) provides information on hazardous materials and wastes. Chemical makers must provide an SDS for each product. Distributors must get the SDS to employers. It must be available to workers exposed to hazardous substances. An SDS is required at greenhouses and nurseries with more than 11 full- or part-time workers. Keep at least one copy of the SDS with the chemical.

What Is in an SDS?

SDSs provide vital information to different people on the job:

- Workers who use, handle, and store hazardous substances.
- Employers who must provide safe storage and appropriate Personal Protection Equipment (PPE).
- Emergency personnel who respond in case of a spill, accident, or physical injury. These can include firefighters, hazardous material crews, and medical personnel.

SDSs are not all the same. They can be organized in a number of different ways. Some SDSs have only eight or nine sections; others may have 12 or 14. However, any SDS should include these types of information:

- Product identification
    1. Formal chemical name and make-up
    2. Trade name on the label
    3. Name and locations of the manufacturer and distributor
    4. Emergency telephone number(s)
- Hazard identification
    1. Amount of hazardous ingredient that causes ill effects
        - Threshold Limit Value (TLV) — maximum average concentration recommended over an eight hour workday.
        - Permissible Exposure Limit (PEL) — exposure limit set by the Occupational Safety and Health Administration (OSHA); enforced by law.
        - Lethal Dose Concentration (LD50) — dose that kills 50 percent of test animals in experiments.
    2. Overview of information for emergency personnel
    3. Ill effects of acute ocular, oral, dermal, or inhalation exposure
    4. Chronic effects of long-term exposure
- First-aid procedures
    1. What to do in case of acute exposure
    2. Instructions to medical personnel for emergency procedures
- Handling and storage procedures
    1. Hygiene
    2. Temperature control
    3. Ventilation
- Personal Protection Equipment (PPE)
    1. Personal eye protection to avoid ocular exposure
    2. Rubber gloves, rubber boots, long-sleeve shirt, long pants, and face shields to avoid dermal exposure
    3. Respiratory protection to avoid inhalation exposure
- Fire and explosion hazards and procedures
- Procedures for cleaning up spills and leaks
- Disposal information

How to Use an SDS

- Find out where SDSs are kept in your workplace. Find out how they are filed so you can find the one you want.

- Look over the format of each SDS to see how information is presented.
- Find out how to make the SDS available to emergency personnel, if necessary.
- Find out what PPE is required to handle the substance.
- Find out what procedures are needed for safe handling — hygiene, temperature control, ventilation.
- Look for information on ill effects of acute exposure. Find out what symptoms you should look for when you handle the substance.
- Find out what first aid procedures to use for acute exposure.
- Find out how to handle a spill or a leak.
- Find out how to store the substance safely when you finish the job.
- Ask your supervisor any questions you still have about how to handle the substance safely.

Employer Training

Employers must provide information and training to workers who might be exposed to hazardous chemicals. New workers must be trained before they first work with a hazardous chemical. And all workers must be trained when a new hazard is introduced to the workplace. All workers should find out what training their employer provides. They should also make sure they receive all the training they need.

Review These Important Points

- The SDS provides critical details about the substance it describes.
- The SDS lists hazardous ingredients and other health hazards.
- The SDS identifies Personal Protection Equipment required for the substance.
- Workers must receive training on hazardous chemicals.

Topic:		
Instructor:	Location:	
Printed Name	**Signature**	**Date**

Topic: No Riders on Lawn Equipment

Most equipment does not have an extra seat, but some workers allow riders. **Any rider for any reason is a safety hazard.** An extra rider may block the driver's view or movement. And a rider also may:

- Fall from the equipment.
- Be run over.
- Become entangled in equipment.
- Be killed.

Extra passengers are problematic because they:

- Interfere with the operator's vision and ability to use controls.
- Distract the operator.
- Increase the rider's exposure to noise, dust, and chemicals.
- Increase the risk of a multiple injury incident.

Advance planning helps avoid the need for riders. You can plan other transportation if additional workers are needed at the work site.

Remember

- Only one person is allowed on each piece of machinery.
- No riders should be allowed on any lawn equipment. This should be strictly enforced. No children —ever!
- New workers should be trained in the classroom or the shop before they drive machinery and lawn equipment.
- Use additional vehicles to transport workers to and from a job site — not lawn equipment.

Review These Important Points

- Riders on any power equipment are a safety hazard and should not be allowed.
- All drivers of equipment need training in a classroom setting.
- Plan transportation for passengers early. This reduces the temptation to carry riders on machinery and lawn equipment.

Topic:		
Instructor:	Location:	
Printed Name	**Signature**	**Date**

Topic: Shoveling Snow

Shoveling snow is a straightforward process, but it is a work task that often ends in injury both on the job and at home. The American Journal of Emergency Medicine conducted a study that looked at the most common health hazards when shoveling snow. They looked at 195,000 injuries treated at hospitals that resulted from shoveling snow over a 17-year period (1990-2006).

Among the study findings:

- Overworking your muscles, falling, and being hit with the shovel were the most common reasons for getting injured.
- Muscle, ligament, tendon, and other soft tissue injuries topped the list of snow shoveling mishaps. Lower back injuries were common.
- Other common snow shoveling injuries included cuts and broken bones. The arms and hands were the most likely body regions to sustain a bone fracture.
- Heart-related problems made up only 7% of snow shoveling injuries. However, all deaths due to snow shoveling were caused by heart problems.
- Adults over 55 were over four times more likely than younger people to have heart-related symptoms while shoveling.

Best Practices to Avoid Injury While Shoveling Snow

- Prior to considering shoveling as your only option, consider mechanical methods to clear snow, such as a vehicle with a plow or snowblower.
- If you do have to shovel, take time to warm up or properly stretch prior to starting.
- Do not overexert yourself. If you are not used to a heavy physical workload or have health issues take your time while shoveling snow. Depending on the severity of any health issues, consider eliminating shoveling altogether by having someone else complete the task.
- Use proper work posture when shoveling. Avoid actions such as rounding your back or twisting when lifting.
- Always lift with your legs and not with your back.
- When possible, push the snow out of the way to limit lifting and throwing the snow. Pushing the snow is less hazardous than lifting and throwing snow.
- Use an ergonomically friendly snow shovel. While the overall design of snow shovels is basically the same, there are many that have been designed with the human body in mind.
- Watch your step and ensure you are wearing the proper footwear for the task. Preventing slips, trips, and falls in winter weather conditions can be extremely difficult to do. Having the proper footwear and taking your time while walking can reduce the chance of these incidents occurring.

Summary

While the task of shoveling snow is a straightforward one, there are many injuries that can occur while performing this task. Consider the injuries mentioned in this talk and the steps you can take to avoid an injury the next time you have to shovel snow.

Discussion point: What other hazards and best practices are there when shoveling snow?

Topic:		
Instructor:	Location:	
Printed Name	**Signature**	**Date**

Topic: Overhead Electrical Hazards

Long, tall, or large equipment can come in contact with overhead power lines:

- Ladders
- Long-handled trim saws
- Portable elevators
- Augers
- Irrigation pipes
- Dump trucks

When equipment contacts power lines, workers can be electrocuted and badly injured, even killed. Irrigation pipes and other machinery only need to be near an overhead power line to kill.

Check the Location of Overhead Power Lines

- Pulling or installing pump casing and pipe
- Raising or lowering machines
- Moving irrigation pipes
- Raising or moving ladders
- Pruning trees from the ground
- Working in trees
- Constructing buildings
- Performing building maintenance

Remember These Cautions

- **Always look up for overhead hazards** like power lines, especially high-voltage lines.
- Always assume that overhead power lines don't have protective insulation, so any contact is dangerous.
- Work as a team. One worker on the ground should be on the lookout for possible contact between equipment and power lines.
- Nonmetallic materials can conduct electricity. These are lumber, tree limbs, tires, and ropes.
- Electricity seeks one or more paths of least resistance. This includes going **through** people.
- Do not touch power lines.
- Untrained workers must stay at least 10 feet away from unguarded equipment.
- Never store anything under power lines — no equipment, no tools, no vehicles, no materials, nothing.
- Stay away from fallen overhead wires. Notify the power company right away.
- Ladders should not be used near overhead power lines.
- Plan a travel route for equipment that avoids overhead power lines.
- The ground level should not be raised under overhead power lines.

If You Are in a Vehicle That Comes into Contact With a Power Line

- Most important, **stay in the vehicle or in the boom or crane.** Do not try to get out unless the vehicle is on fire.
- If you can, disconnect from the power line. Back the vehicle or swing the boom or crane away from the power line.
- Get help from the power company — use your cell phone to call or yell to others nearby. Make sure no one else approaches the vehicle.
- Do not leave the vehicle until the power company tells you the line is de-energized. You can never know for sure if the line is going to come back on or not.

- **If the vehicle catches on fire, exit the vehicle very carefully:**
  - o Jump out of the vehicle. Don't worry about how far you jump, as long as you clear the vehicle.
  - o Be sure to land on both feet and keep your balance when you land. This is more important than how far away you jump.
  - o Don't touch anything with your hands; use your hands for balance only.
  - o Keep both feet on the ground at all times. Hop away from the vehicle — be sure to keep both feet together. Use your hands for balance only.
  - o If you cannot hop, shuffle away — and keep both feet on the ground at all times. Do not lift one foot off the ground to step forward. Instead, drag one foot forward keeping it in touch with the ground.
  - o Keep hopping or shuffling away until you get to where other people are standing safely.

Review These Important Points
- Assume overhead power lines have no protective insulation and contact may be fatal.
- Work as a team. One worker on the ground spots for the worker on raised equipment.
- Electricity always seeks one or more paths of least resistance.
- Never touch fallen overhead wires. Notify the power company right away.
- Workers should check for overhead power lines before doing any work.
- Plan your route of travel to avoid power lines.

Topic:		
Instructor:	Location:	

Printed Name	Signature	Date

Topic: Personal Eye Protection

Shatterproof safety glasses, safety goggles, and face shields offer eye and face protection. And yet they provide for clear vision. Many eye protectors also have side shields and/or filter lenses. Side shields offer protection from flying objects. However, eye protection may not stop high-velocity flying objects. Filter lenses provide protection from radiation such as is encountered in welding.

.

As of July 5, 1994, all safety glasses must meet the minimum standards set forth by the American National Standards Institute (ANSI). Approved lenses are marked by the manufacturer. ANSI standard Z87.2 is for high impact protection. ANSI standard Z87.1 is for general eye and face protection, including chemical splash protection.

Workers who wear prescription glasses should wear additional protective eyewear. Protective eyewear can either incorporate prescription lenses or fit comfortably over prescription glasses without disturbing the fit.

Select Protective Eyewear
- Wear goggles or a face shield around hazards:
  - Flying chips or particles
  - Electrical arcing or sparks
  - Chemical gases or vapors
  - Harmful light
  - Liquid chemicals, acids, or caustics (e.g., fertilizer solutions, acids used to lower water pH, pesticides, or growth regulators)
  - Molten metal
  - Dust
  - Swinging objects like ropes or chains.
- Goggles only provide eye protection. Face shields provide protection for the whole face.
- Be certain that protective eyewear is approved protection against the hazard for which it is being used. For example, workers need impact resistance for protection against flying objects. They need chemical splash resistance when working with liquid chemicals.
- If filter lenses are used, be certain that the filter lens is of a shade number appropriate for the type of work.
- Check with suppliers for the most appropriate types of eye protection for the hazard.

Inspect Protective Eyewear
- The arm pieces on safety glasses should touch the side of the head and curl behind the ears.
- Goggle lenses should be centered. The strap should rest low on the back of the head.
- Flexible elastic headbands must be in good shape.
- Discard pitted or scratched eyewear. Eyewear should be clean and defogged.
- Protective eyewear should fit snugly. It should be reasonably comfortable under conditions of use.

Keep Protective Eyewear Clean
- Clean the lenses thoroughly with soap and water.
- Disinfect eyewear that has been exposed to a hazardous substance or worn by someone else.
- Store clean eye wear in a closed, dustproof case. Plastic bags with a zipper work well.

To Protect the Eyes, Follow These Safety Tips
- Turn containers away from the face when opening.
- Remove protective eyewear only after turning off the tool.

- Replace outdated or scratched prescription lenses; they can distort vision.
- Replace cracked, pitted, or damaged goggles or spectacles.
- Concentrate on the task at hand when using power tools.
- Stop and relax the eyes if they are becoming strained.
- Keep sharp or pointed objects away from the face and eyes.

Review These Important Points
- Tools should be turned off before removing goggles.
- Inspect eyewear before wearing.
- Protective eyewear must comply with the minimum requirements of the American National Standards Institute.
- Store eyewear in a clean, dustproof case.
- Clean eye wear regularly.

Topic:		
Instructor:	Location:	
Printed Name	**Signature**	**Date**

Topic: Pesticide Exposure

There are four ways you can be exposed to pesticides:

- **Oral exposure** — swallowing pesticide
- **Dermal exposure** — getting pesticide on your skin, the most common type
- **Inhalation exposure** — breathing in pesticide
- **Ocular exposure** — getting pesticide in your eye

Causes for each type of exposure are explained here.

Type of Exposure	Cause of Exposure
Oral Exposure	• Not washing hands before eating, drinking, using tobacco. • Eating or drinking a pesticide by mistake. • Getting pesticide on food. • Splashing pesticide into the mouth. • Blowing out plugged nozzles with the mouth.
Dermal Exposure	• Getting pesticides on bare skin. • Applying pesticides in windy weather. • Wearing inadequate PPE.
Inhalation Exposure	• Prolonged contact in poorly ventilated areas. • Not using proper PPE. • Breathing vapors after application. • Using the wrong respirator. • Using an improperly fitted respirator. • Using tainted filters, cartridges, or canisters.
Ocular Exposure	• Getting pesticides in the eyes. • Not using proper eye cover when: • Spraying pesticide • Handling pesticide • Rubbing the eye with tainted gloves or hands.

Acute and Chronic Exposure

Exposure is **acute** if you are exposed to a large amount of pesticide once. A spill on the body is one example. It's usually easy to identify acute exposure.

Exposure is **chronic** if you have low-level exposure over and over. Chronic exposure may be hard to tell. Either kind of exposure is dangerous. But a combination of acute and chronic exposure can be especially dangerous. For example:

- Wearing contaminated clothing can cause chronic exposure.
- A worker with chronic exposure might spill a pesticide on the skin.
- Now the worker has both chronic and acute exposure.
- The body may not be able to deal with the acute exposure on top of the chronic exposure. The worker is at great risk.

To Avoid Exposure

- Read pesticide labels. Look for the types of PPE needed and emergency procedures.
- Wear proper PPE.

- Wear proper eye cover.
- Use respirators whenever needed.
- If you breathe a pesticide, move away from the area quickly. Get to fresh air.
- Use a closed handling system. This keeps the applicator separate from the pesticide and avoids exposure.
- Maintain and clean PPE.
- Launder clothing after handling pesticides.
- Wash exposed body parts often to reduce dermal exposure.
- In case of exposure:
    - Use showers, eyewash fountains, hand/face spray units, and other emergency equipment.
    - Call 911 if appropriate.
    - Report exposure.

Review These Important Points
- In dermal exposure, pesticide gets on the skin.
- In ocular exposure, the pesticide gets in the eye.
- In oral exposure, pesticide is swallowed.
- In inhalation exposure, pesticide is breathed in.
- You can be exposed to a pesticide if you use improper PPE.

Topic:		
Instructor:	Location:	
Printed Name	**Signature**	**Date**

Topic: Hand Injury Prevention

 We use our hands for virtually every task we do at work and because of this fact they are commonly injured on the job. Keeping our hands and fingers out of harm's way at work is critical. A serious injury to an individual's hands or fingers results in a huge negative impact on their ability to work and overall quality of life. While gloves are the most common form of PPE found in the workplace, hand injuries are still the second leading type of injury on the job.

Hand Injury Statistics

- There are 110,000 lost time cases due to hand injuries annually.
- 1 million workers are treated in an ER for hand injuries annually.
- 70% of workers who experienced a hand injury were not wearing gloves.
- Another 30% of victims had gloves on, but they were damaged or inadequate for the work task.

Three Common Types of Hand Injuries

1. Lacerations are the most common type of hand injuries. Lacerations are due to sharp objects or tools. Often inadequate gloves are used during an activity that involves a sharp tool. A glove with Kevlar is effective in protecting the hand against a cutting or slicing motion. A straight stab motion can still easily penetrate these gloves. Caution needs to be used when using any tool that can easily penetrate the skin.

2. Crush injuries are usually due to employees placing their hands in the line of fire between two objects or in a rotating piece of equipment. Pinch points on equipment or tools also commonly lead to crush injuries.

3. Fractures occur when there is a sudden blow to the bones in the fingers or hands. Motor vehicle accidents often cause fractures to the hands. Another common cause of fractures is an individual extending out their hands to catch themselves from a fall.

Safe Work Practices

- Use tools to remove your hands from the line of fire when doing a work task that could result in injury to your hands or fingers. Using tools such as push sticks when using a table saw is an example that removes your hands from the line of fire.

- Avoid using fixed open blade knives. There are safety knives that limit the length of the blade exposed. They also have a safety feature that retracts the blade when pressure is let off the handle or switch that controls the blade.

- Never put your hand in an area where you cannot see it.

- Always wear the proper gloves for whatever work task you are doing. Understand the limitations of your gloves and what work tasks they are appropriate for.

Discussion points:

- What are some of the biggest hazards to our hands onsite?
- Next time you are doing a simple task at home such as setting the table for dinner, getting ready in the morning, or cleaning- try doing the task with one or two less fingers. It sounds like a silly exercise, but this can help put into perspective how hard it would be to complete tasks without some of our fingers. It is easy to take for granted our health and abilities when we have had them for so long.

Topic:		
Instructor:	Location:	
Printed Name	**Signature**	**Date**

Topic: Poison Ivy, Poison Oak, and Poison Sumac

Many people are sensitive to poison ivy, poison oak, and
poison sumac. A chemical called urushiol is present in
the sap of these plants. If you touch or brush against a
plant with broken stems or torn leaves, the sap can
come into contact with your skin. The sap can cause a
rash, blisters, and itching. Urushiol can stay on clothing,
gloves, and tools for years if they are not washed.

Poison Ivy   Poison Sumac   Poison Oak

How to Avoid Contact with Poison Ivy, Poison Oak, and Poison Sumac

- Recognize the leaf pattern of these poisonous plants and avoid them if possible.
- Try not to touch or brush against these plants.
- Dress appropriately. Wear gloves, a cap, a long-sleeve shirt, and long pants. Wear boots or shoes. Do not wear sandals or open-toed shoes.
- At the end of the workday, do not take a bath. Urushiol can stay in the tub water and can cling to your body when you get out of the tub. Instead, take a shower.
- Wash all your work clothes and gloves in hot water. Do not wash them with other clothes.
- Wash off tools with an outdoor water hose.
- Do not burn the plant. Burning can release the chemical in the smoke, and it can come into contact with your skin that way.

How to Treat a Poisonous Reaction

- If you know you have been exposed to urushiol, use rubbing alcohol on the exposed skin immediately. Once urushiol comes in contact with your skin, it penetrates very quickly. Also, do not return to the area where you were exposed until the next day. Rubbing alcohol removes the protective barrier on your skin and if you should contact urushiol again, it will penetrate your skin even faster.
- After using the rubbing alcohol, wash the exposed area with water.
- As soon as possible, shower with warm water and soap or a special wash like Zanfel™.
- All clothing should be washed separately in hot water. Shoes should be wiped with rubbing alcohol and water. Wear disposable gloves while cleaning your shoes.

If a Rash, Blisters, or Itching Develops

- A rash or blisters may develop if the skin is not cleaned quickly. This redness or swelling usually occurs within 12 to 48 hours after contact.
- Oozing blisters are not contagious because they do not contain urushiol. The fluid cannot spread the rash to other parts of the body. However, do not rub or scratch the blisters or rash. Infection could occur if your hands or fingernails are dirty.
- You will only have a rash or blisters where urushiol touched your body. The rash will not spread by itself. However, you might get a rash in a new area if you handle contaminated items again.
- The rash and blisters may appear at different times because the poison may absorb into your skin at different rates of penetration, depending on what part of the body was exposed.
- If you do nothing, the rash, blisters, and itch will go away in two to three weeks.
- If you want to treat the rash, blisters, and itch, try putting wet compresses on the area or soaking in cool water.
- To ease the itching, you can take oral antihistamines or hydrocortisones. These pills can be purchased at a local pharmacy.

- If you have a severe reaction, see a doctor. The doctor may prescribe an oral corticosteroid especially if the rash is on a sensitive part of the body. The drug must be taken for at least two to three weeks. If you stop too soon, the rash can reappear and be even worse.
- These over-the-counter products may also help dry oozing blisters: aluminum acetate, baking soda, Aveeno, aluminum hydroxide gel, calamine, kaolin, zinc acetate, zinc carbonate, and zinc oxide. Follow the directions on the label.

Review These Important Points

- While you are working, try not to touch poisonous plants.
- Usushiol can remain on your clothes for years if they are not washed properly.
- When working around poisonous plants, wear clothing that covers as much of your body as possible.
- Do not burn poisonous plants. Burning can release the poison into the air.
- Use rubbing alcohol immediately if you come into contact with a poisonous plant.
- Shower with warm water and soap as soon as possible.
- Wash your clothes separately in hot water. Clean your shoes with alcohol and water.
- If you develop a rash, blisters, and itching, apply warm compresses to the infected areas or bathe in cool water.
- Try using over-the-counter products to help ease the itch. Follow the directions on the label.
- If you have a severe reaction, see a doctor.

Topic:		
Instructor:	Location:	
Printed Name	**Signature**	**Date**

Topic: Power Lawn Mowers Safety

A power lawn mower can be dangerous and cause serious injuries. A rotary mower blade whirls at 2,000 and 4,000 revolutions per minute. The tip of the blade travels at 100 to 200 miles per hour. For safety reasons, it is important to know how to quickly disengage the clutch and stop the engine.

To Operate *Any* Power Lawn Mower, Follow These Tips

- Begin by reading the operator's manual.
- Before mowing, remove debris from lawn.
- Wear protective, close-fitting clothing.
- Use hearing protection if indicated by the operator's manual.
- Take mowers out of gear before starting.
- Keep all guards and safety shields in place.
- Never disengage any safety interlock switch.
- Never fill the gasoline tank on the mower if the engine is hot.
- Store gasoline in an approved, properly labeled container.
- Never store gasoline or any other hazardous material in a food container.
- Turn off the motor before removing a foreign object.
- Disconnect the spark or electric plug before repairing mower.
- Provide routine maintenance.
- Warn humans and pets to stay away from operating mowers.

Tip for Push Mowers

- Start push mowers from a firm stance with feet in a safe position.

Tip for Electric Mowers

- Never use an electric mower on wet grass.

Tips for Riding Mowers

- Keep both feet on the footrests of a riding mower.
- Turn off the motor before dismounting.
- No extra riders on self-propelled mowers.
- Be aware of power-take-offs.

Be Aware of Mowing Hazards

- A mower can tip over easily.
- Push the mower away from the body during a fall.
- Never leave a running mower unattended.
- Take rest periods as needed.
- Foreign objects can fly from the mower, so make sure the mowing area, including the throwing distance of the blade, is clear of people and animals.

Proper Mowing Directions

- When mowing on a slope with a riding mower, you should mow down the slope.
- When mowing on a slope with a push mower, you should mow across the slope.

Proper Dress for Mowing

- Sturdy shoes are a must; steel-toed work boots are advised.

- Long pants and long-sleeve shirts protect from flying debris, grass clippings, and sun.
- Safety glasses or goggles, especially when mowing near solid objects like gravel driveways.
- Hearing protection may be necessary.

Review These Important Points

- A rotary blade whirls between 2,000 and 4,000 revolutions per minute, with top speeds between 100 to 200 miles per hour.
- Wear protective, snug clothing when mowing.
- Keep guards and safety shields in place.
- Never disengage any safety interlock switch.
- Turn off the mower before removing any foreign objects.
- Know how to disengage the clutch and stop the engine.
- Never leave a running mower unattended.

Topic:		
Instructor:	Location:	
Printed Name	**Signature**	**Date**

Topic: Personal Protective Equipment for Pesticides

Different Personal Protection Equipment (PPE) is available for use with pesticides. Pesticide labels give minimum requirements. The Environmental Protection Agency (EPA) provides resistance ratings for equipment. Remember that more is better!

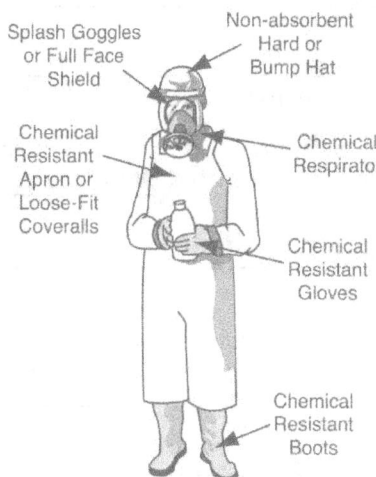

Gloves

Wear unlined, elbow length, chemical-resistant gloves when handling any pesticide concentrate or chemical labeled DANGER, POISON, or WARNING. Not all gloves are suitable for all chemicals. Contact the glove manufacturer to determine if a specific glove is suitable for a particular chemical.
Check gloves for holes or leaks. To check for leaks, fill the gloves with water and squeeze. Throw the gloves away if water squirts through a hole. Leaks or holes in the gloves can expose the skin to chemicals. Either tuck gloves into shirt sleeves or vice versa. This prevents the chemicals from getting inside the gloves at the cuff. Before removing the gloves, wash them with detergent and water to prevent contaminating the hands.
Never wear cotton or leather gloves. They do not protect against skin exposure. Instead, they absorb the pesticide; workers are exposed again each time they wear the gloves.

Footwear

Wear unlined, lightweight, nonabsorbent boots that go up to mid calf. Wear long pants over boots to avoid getting pesticides inside the boots. After each use, thoroughly wash and dry boots inside and out to remove residue. Always wear gloves when cleaning contaminated footwear or any equipment.

Eye Protection

Wear tight fitting, non-fogging chemical splash goggles or a full face shield with splash protection. Straps should be nonabsorbent. Clean the eye protection and wash the sweatband after each use.

Head Protection

Wear a waterproof rain hat or washable, wide-brimmed hard or bump hat. Or, wear the hood of a disposable suit. Avoid cotton and felt hats — no ball caps. They absorb pesticides; workers are exposed again when they wear the hat again.

Clothing

Spraying contaminates clothing so be sure to wear fresh clothing daily. Remove contaminated clothing starting at the top and moving down. Roll clothing off, rolling contamination inward to prevent spreading. Wash contaminated clothing separately from other laundry. Dispose of hooded disposable suits and items that are saturated with pesticides. Drop into plastic waste bag rolled in an open position.

Respirators

Wear a respirator when the pesticide label recommends it. It will be necessary to wear a respirator when handling concentrated, highly toxic pesticides. Be sure that the respirator fits properly and is the appropriate type for the hazard. Wear only respirators approved by the National Institute for Occupational Safety and Health (NIOSH) with the correct filter.

Review These Important Points

- Wear the right equipment for the job.
- Never use faulty or worn-out equipment.
- Always wash thoroughly when finished with pesticide applications.

Topic:

Instructor: Location:

Printed Name	Signature	Date

Topic: Preventing Lifting and Overexertion Injuries

Approximately 25 percent of workplace injuries result from lifting, pulling, or pushing objects. The part of the body most often injured is the back.

Material Handling — Think Before Lifting

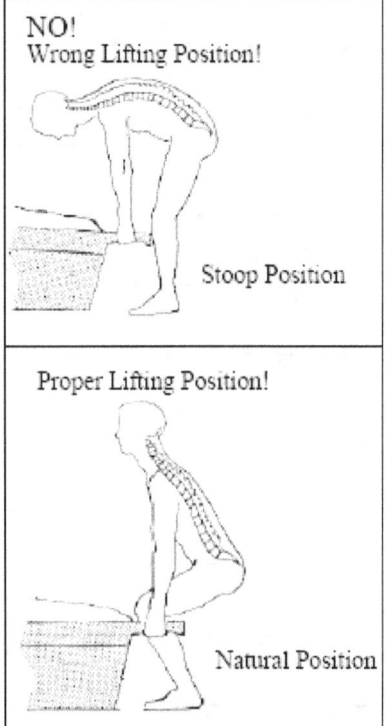

- Arrange your package delivery and material handling systems so that heavy loads are lifted and carried near the waist, between knee height and shoulder height.
- When possible, set heavy objects on pallets, benches, or other supports near waist height — not on the ground. It is impossible to achieve a good back position when lifting heavy objects from the ground.
- Have a handling plan that avoids slippery hazards and includes a destination.
- Test the load to be sure that it can be safely carried.
- Know the limits! If the load is too heavy, awkward, or bulky to carry alone, get help.
- Use machinery or equipment, such as a pushcart, hand truck, wheelbarrow, forklift, or hoist.
- Do not overlook the use of levers, inclined planes, or rollers to move loads. Serious back injuries occur because of improper lifting techniques, like these:
- Bending from the waist to pick up objects.
- Lifting boxes above the chest.
- Twisting the body to carry or lift a heavy box or object.
- Lifting objects when in poor physical condition.

Guidelines for Safe Lifting

- **Use a proper lifting position.** Lift with your knees and legs — not with your back.
- **Get a good grip.** Grasp the load firmly. Use gloves if they allow for a better grip.
- **Get a good footing.** Center body weight to provide a powerful line of thrust and good balance.
- **Keep it close.** Grasp the load firmly and lift towards the belt buckle. Hold the load close to the body to avoid putting pressure on the back.
- **Lift smoothly.** Raise, carry, and lower the load smoothly. Never jerk a load.
- **Avoid twisting.** If turning is required while lifting or carrying a load, move the feet to turn the body instead of twisting at the waist.
- **Push.** Push rather than pull the load.

Review These Important Points

- Approximately 25 percent of work-related injuries result from overexertion, mainly from lifting.
- Think and plan before lifting.
- Push rather than pull the load.
- Use mechanical means whenever possible.
- Avoid twisting when lifting or setting down a load. Move the feet to turn the body instead of twisting at the waist.

Topic:		
Instructor:	Location:	
Printed Name	**Signature**	**Date**

Topic: Preventing Falls from Trees

You should always use a full-body harness and other safety equipment while working in trees. A full-body harness wraps around the waist, shoulders, and legs. It has a D-ring in the center of the back to attach a lanyard or other safety devices. A full-body harness is the best type of safety system to use while you are trimming limbs. Always secure the harness before you start. Ask your employer if training and safety classes are provided for the proper use of harnesses and trimming equipment such as chain saws, hand cutting saws, and pruners. A safety belt can also be used while trimming limbs in trees. However, a safety belt will only keep you in position.

It will not protect you if you should fall.

While trimming tree limbs, always be aware of electrical power lines. Most power lines are not insulated. Serious injury and possible electrocution can occur if you come into contact with power lines. Only experienced workers should trim trees near power lines. If possible, your employer should ask the power company to cut the power while you are trimming trees near power lines.

Overhead Power Lines
- **Check for overhead power lines!**
- Stay at least 10 feet away from power lines.

Safety Procedures to Prevent Falls
- Check trees and tree limbs for structural weakness before you climb or start trimming.
- Check all equipment for defects before you climb or start trimming.
- Be sure you are properly tied into the tree before you start trimming.
- Use a safety rope to raise and lower tools.
- Always pay attention to your footing. Check before you change your position.
- Always make sure that other workers are not below while you are trimming.
- If possible, have a co-worker on the ground act as a spotter.
- Do not work in trees if you are tired. Fatigue can lead to a fall or an accident.

Safety Equipment
- Full-body safety harness
- Safety belt
- Lanyards
- Lifelines
- Cross-arm strap
- Earplugs or noise mufflers
- Safety glasses or goggles
- Gloves
- Hard hat
- Steel-toed boots

Review These Important Points
- Always use the proper safety equipment while pruning trees to lessen the possibility of falling or having an accident.
- Only experienced workers should trim or prune tree limbs near power lines.
- Check all equipment for defects before you climb or start trimming.
- Never use a metal ladder to trim tree limbs near power lines.

Topic:		
Instructor:	Location:	

Printed Name	Signature	Date

Topic: Preventing Falls

Falls can cause serious injuries, as well as damage to facilities and equipment. Workers can fall off things or fall into openings. They can trip over obstructions or lose their footing on slippery surfaces. Some basic guidelines can help prevent falls.

Housekeeping

- Add rubber mats to smooth-finished concrete floors.
- Clean up spills immediately.
- Use absorbent material to reduce slipping.
- Dry floors prevent slipping.
- Be alert to potential problems like:
    - Wet floors
    - Tangled or loose hoses
    - Moss or algae on floors
    - Mix of water and growth media
- Be aware of the work environment, personal safety, and the safety of co-workers.

Floor Openings

Floor openings should be guarded by a standard fixed railing on all exposed sides. Consider using a sturdy hinged floor opening cover with removable standard railings on all exposed sides in high traffic areas. Workers should use an access ladder to get up on scaffolds; they should not climb the side of the scaffold.

Ladders

- Use a ladder with two side rails joined by regularly spaced steps, rungs, or cleats, allowing for up and down movement.
- Never extend the body outside the ladder side rails.

Four-to-One Rule:

For every 4 feet of rise, the base of the ladder should be 1 foot away from the object the ladder is resting against.

- Use the Four-to-One Rule to place the ladder. Place the bottom of the ladder 1/4 of its vertical height from the building (i.e., 4 feet for 16-foot ladder).
- The top of a lean-to ladder should be 36 inches higher than the level at which the employee is working.
- Do **not** stand on the top two rungs of a stepladder.
- Observe the location of electrical wires. Stay clear of electrical lines and lighting fixtures.
- Keep metal ladders away from electrical wires.
- Watch out for movable equipment like portable benches or traveling booms.

Scaffolding

Scaffolds are temporary, elevated platforms used for supporting workers and/or materials. Scaffolds must have guardrails and toe boards. Guardrails are a barrier secured to uprights and erected along the exposed sides and ends of platforms to prevent falls.

Mobile Scissors Lifts

Greenhouse and nursery workers often use mobile scissors lifts in performing their jobs. If you use this type of equipment, be sure to follow the equipment safety instructions.

- Make sure all handrails and other safety devices are in place and operating.
- Be aware of other workers in the work area.

- Be aware of uneven surfaces as you move the lift.
- Be aware of beams, trusses, and gutters that may be below head level.

Stairs

- Walk — don't run — when using stairways.
- Use handrails.
- Open, exposed stairs should have a railing. Handrails should be provided on at least one side of closed stairways, preferably on the right side descending.
- Uncluttered stairways with good tread are safest.

General Tips to Prevent Falls

- You are more likely to slip when rushed or distracted, so do not run.
- Avoid rapid changes of direction.
- Keep floors in good repair.
- Wear shoes with pliable soles and low heels.
- Close open drawers, cabinets, doors, or closets after use.
- Watch out for movable equipment like portable benches or traveling booms.

Review These Important Points

- Keeping the work area free of spills helps prevent slips and falls.
- All open spaces should have a fixed railing around them.
- Always use an approved ladder.
- Scaffolding must have guardrails and toe boards.

Topic:		
Instructor:	Location:	
Printed Name	**Signature**	**Date**

Topic: Preventing Machine Hazards

There are thousands of machine-related injuries each year. Proper training can prevent these injuries. Workers should know how to operate a piece of machinery and inspect for problem areas before turning on the power. Keeping air hoses and extension cords out of the way reduces tripping hazards.

Check Before Operating

- Have you reviewed the owner's manual? It will provide operating, repairing, lubricating, and fuel information.
- Are the Warning decals in place?
- Are the machine guards properly placed and in good condition?
- Are electrical lines damage free?
- Are air and hydraulic lines in good condition and not leaking?
- Is the setup a proper setup?
- Is the area around the machines orderly?
- Is the equipment jack in working order?

Personal Protection

- Wear Personal Protection Equipment, such as goggles, safety shoes, and leather gloves.
- Long hair should be tied back or tucked under to avoid getting caught in machinery.
- Avoid wearing jewelry.

Machine Maintenance Safety Checklist

- Keep machines repaired, lubricated, and adjusted.
- Clean up excess lubricants.
- Clearly mark control switches and valves that control machines.
- Check machines for emergency stop switches; they should be located on or near the machine so the machine can be turned off quickly if a malfunction occurs.

During Operation

- Turn power off and remove the key before working around or performing maintenance on the machine.
- Use appropriate lockout and tagout procedures to prevent equipment from being re-energized while work is being performed on or around it.
- Stay away from moving parts.

Review These Important Points

- Always wear PPE on the job.
- Avoid wearing jewelry, hair styles, or loose clothing that might get caught on machinery.
- Keep work space clutter free.
- Know how to use the machine safely before operating.

Topic:		
Instructor:	Location:	
Printed Name	**Signature**	**Date**

Topic: Ergonomic Back Pain

Ergonomic injury risk factors include forceful movements, repetitive motions, awkward postures, and lack of rest. Rest periods give the body time to recover from work; breaktime exercises and stretches strengthen the body. Workers should think of themselves as Industrial Athletes; athletes wouldn't participate in a sport without proper rest and warm-up, so use the same preparation on the job.

Maintaining overall health reduces your risk of injury. Get a good night's sleep to rest your body and maintain alertness. Eat healthy foods and drink fluids to boost energy and stay hydrated. Aerobic exercise and weight training increase strength and vitality. Stretching, yoga, and pilates improve flexibility and build core body strength.

Pay attention to signs of discomfort and fatigue on the job; these are warning signs from your body. As muscles tire during a work task, slouching can lead to poor posture, sloppy, uncontrolled movements, and injuries. Rest breaks mean recovery for the body. During a job task, take micro-breaks lasting 10-15 seconds every ten minutes. Take mini-breaks lasting 3-5 minutes every thirty to sixty minutes. These short breaks give the body a rest, reduce discomfort, and improve your performance.

Alternate your work activities and postures throughout the day. Rotating tasks may seem inefficient, but the rest and use of different muscle groups increases energy and maintains productivity. For example, if you are a landscaper, don't trim all of the shrubs, sweep up the trimmings, and then leaf-blow the whole area; work in sections and trim, sweep, and leaf-blow in alternating tasks. If you work at a single workstation and job task all day, move into different postures while you work: first standing, then standing with one foot resting on a stool, then sitting.

Stretches help you warm-up before work and relax during breaks; they increase flexibility and boost blood flow and oxygen to muscles. Perform stretches slowly and gently; avoid extreme postures and stop stretching if you feel pain or discomfort. Physical and Occupational Therapists are the most qualified individuals to generate a specific stretching and warm-up program.

Overall fitness and flexibility, adequate sleep, task rotation, and rest breaks can help limit the overall risk of injury.

Topic:		
Instructor:	Location:	
Printed Name	**Signature**	**Date**

Topic: Proper Use of Ladders

Most ladder accidents happen when someone falls from a ladder or when the ladder falls because it is being used incorrectly.

Before Climbing a Ladder

- Consider the type of work to be done when choosing a ladder.
- Be certain the ladder is able to carry the amount of weight that will be applied. Check ladder ratings for weight allowed.
  - **Industrial.** Heavy-duty with a load capacity of not more than 250 pounds.
  - **Commercial.** Medium-duty with a load capacity of not more than 225 pounds (suited for painting).
  - **Household.** Light-duty with a load capacity of 200 pounds.
- Check the condition of the ladder using the Ladder Inspection Checklist on the next page.
- Make sure the ladder is placed on a firm, level, slip-free surface away from things like algae growth, oil droplets, potting mix, or wet grass clippings.
- **Check for overhead power lines** outdoors and remain clear of them.
- Check for lighting fixtures indoors and remain clear of them.

Ladder Inspection Checklist								
Metal Ladders	**OK**	**Not OK**	**Wood Ladders**	**OK**	**Not OK**	**Fiberglass Ladders**	**OK**	**Not OK**
Sharp edges?			Splits?			Loose Components?		
Dents?			Cracks?			Missing Components?		
Bent Steps or stiles?			Chips?			Cracks?		
Condition of no-slip or slip-resistant rubber or plastic feet?			Loose steps or rungs?			Chips?		
Corrosion?			Warping?					

Step Ladders

- Be certain the spreader is locked before climbing on the ladder.
- Never stand on the top of a stepladder.
- Note: The top is not a step!

Extension and Straight Ladders

- Raise the extension ladder to the desired height and lock both sides.
- Never stand on the top three rungs of a straight or extension ladder.
- Don't lean a ladder against a movable object.
- Always face the ladder and hold onto the side rails with both hands, when going up or down the ladder.

Proper Ladder Placement

The ladder should be placed according to the Four-to-One Rule. First, measure the rise of the ladder — the height from the ground up to the point where the ladder rests against the object. For every 4 feet of rise, the base of the ladder should be 1 foot away from the object. For example, if a 16-foot ladder leans against a wall, its base should be placed 4 feet from the wall. Keep ladders away from power lines.

Remember

- Never use a ladder in a strong wind unless it is tied securely.
- Never use a ladder in front of a door unless the door is locked, blocked, or guarded, and signs are posted.
- Inspect ladders for potential dangers before using.
- Keep your body centered between the rails of the ladder.
- Always have three points of contact while on a ladder — for example, two feet and one hand.
- Never carry tools or materials in your hand when going up or down a ladder. Use a tool belt or apron with a pocket.
- Only one person should be on a ladder at a time.
- If you must work near power lines, always use a wooden or fiberglass ladder. **Never** work with a metal ladder around power lines.

Review These Important Points

- Choose the right ladder for the intended job.
- Know the potential hazards when using a ladder.
- Know the proper placement of ladders.

Topic:		
Instructor:	Location:	

Printed Name	Signature	Date

Topic: Protecting Hands and Fingers

Workers often use machinery with moving parts that can pinch, cut, or crush hands and fingers. Workers can also injure fingers and hands by using them inappropriately as tools. To protect fingers and hands, workers must be aware of a variety of hazards and use safe practices.

Safe Practices for Machinery

- Identify the pinch points, cut points, and crush points on:
  o Mechanically moved loads
  o Loads being lowered
  o Metal drums
- Pinch points, cut points, and crush points are created when two objects move together.
- Keep fingers and hands away from all pinch points, cut points, and crush points!
- Perform maintenance only when tools or machinery are not in operation.
- Know when to wear gloves. Gloves should be worn when exposed to hazards that cause cuts, scrapes, chemical burns or absorption, or injuries. Do not wear loose-fitting gloves around reciprocating or rotating machine parts.
- Allow rotating parts to come to a stop before working on them. Use appropriate lockout and tagout procedures.
- Stop all machinery such as power lawn mowers before attempting to unclog them.
- If guards are removed to perform maintenance, replace them immediately after servicing.
- Do not disengage safety shutoffs on lawn mowers and other power equipment. That defeats the purpose of the shutoff.
- Do not wear jewelry on fingers, ears, eyebrows, navels, etc., when operating or repairing machinery.

Hands and Fingers Are Not Tools!

- Use a tapered punch or other appropriate tool to align the holes in parts.
- Remove fuses with fuse removers, not fingers.
- Do not test the temperatures of gases, liquids, or solids with hands. Burns and reflex damage can occur immediately.
- Keep grinder tool rests adjusted to 1/8-inch gap or less.
- Handle sharp or pointed tools (hatchets, chisels, punches, awls, knives, pruning equipment, and machine blades) carefully.
- Never use fingers to retrieve objects from mower blades, knife blades, or parts moving together, such as a punch press, rotating parts of drill bits, and reciprocating parts of in-running rolls. Use pliers, tweezers, or similar tools.

Review These Important Points

- Avoid using fingers to retrieve objects near saw blades, knife blades, parts moving together, rotating parts, and reciprocating parts.
- Use and maintain guards on moving machinery parts.
- Do not use hands or fingers to test temperatures.
- Handle sharp or pointed tools carefully.
- Watch for pinch points, cut points, and crush points.
- The power transmission, moving parts, and the point of operation on all machinery or tools should be guarded.

Topic:		
Instructor:	Location:	
Printed Name	**Signature**	**Date**

Topic: Power-Take-Off (PTO) Shielding

Workers can be injured or killed if they are caught in a power-take-off (PTO). PTO shields are designed to prevent accidents. But PTO shields cannot work if they are not in place. And PTO shields cannot work if they are damaged.

Use Caution With PTOs

- Disengage the PTO before getting off a tractor. This reduces the chance of slipping or falling onto a rotating shaft or getting caught in a moving part.
- Integral shields should move freely. When the power is off, the shield should easily rotate by hand. Repair damaged shields or bearings immediately.
- Keep the PTO master shield on the PTO power source in place.
- The equipment operator should wear close-fitting clothes and slip-resistant footwear. Rotating parts catch loose clothing easily.
- Never step across a rotating power shaft. Equipment may require the PTO to run at full speed while the operator is working in the vicinity, so it is crucial to always walk around the revolving shaft.
- Never allow children around the equipment or work area.
- Replace damaged or missing shields immediately. If there are questions about the machinery, check with your employer or equipment dealer.

Review These Important Points

- Keep all shields in place at all times except when servicing.
- Replace all shields immediately after servicing a PTO shaft.
- Never step over a working PTO.
- Always disengage the PTO before getting off a tractor.
- Wear close-fitting clothing when working around a PTO.
- Keep children away from a PTO.

Topic:		
Instructor:	Location:	
Printed Name	**Signature**	**Date**

Topic: Reading Pesticide Labels

Before applying pesticides, workers must know what the label says. The label is the law!
The label shows a number of things:

- The chemical formulation
- Signal words: DANGER, WARNING, CAUTION
- Precautionary statements
- Personal Protection Equipment (PPE) statements
- Application method
- Projected length of exposure.

Workers can use pesticides safely and correctly if they read the label.

When to Read the Label

- **Before purchasing the pesticide.** The pesticide must be registered for your intended use. You must make sure there are no restrictions that would prohibit its use.
- **Before mixing and applying the pesticide.** Understand how to mix and safely apply the pesticide. Know the first aid needed if an accident occurs.
- **When storing pesticides.** Pesticides can break down and contaminate storage areas. They are also fire hazards. So they must be stored properly. The pesticide storage center should be securely locked. You should store pesticides by hazard classes:
  - Solvent-based products like Dimethoate 2.67 EC
  - Corrosive alkalis like bleach or lime
  - Corrosive acids like muriatic acids
  - Fertilizers
- **Before disposing of unused pesticide and empty containers.** Workers must prevent environmental contamination and human health hazards. Reduce carryover; buy only what is needed for this season. Try to find a use for all of the pesticide. Never pour pesticides down a drain. Pesticides are hazardous waste. Follow state and federal regulations when you use them and dispose of them.

What Information Does the Label Contain?

- **Brand name.** The name the manufacturer gives to the pesticide.
- **Chemical name.** The name chemists use to describe the chemical structure of the pesticide.
- **Common name.** Most pesticides also have an official common name. For example, horticultural oil is a common name. Common names and brand names are not the same. Not all labels list a common name.
- **Formulation.** Labels always list the formulation type. Some examples are emulsifiable concentrate (EC), wettable powder (WP), or soluble powder (SP).
- **Ingredients.** The label lists the percentage of active and inert ingredients by weight. Inert ingredients do not have pesticidal action.
- **Contents.** The label lists the net contents, by weight or liquid volume, contained in the package.
- **Manufacturer.** The label always lists the name and address of the manufacturer.
- **Registration and Establishment Numbers.** The Environmental Protection Agency (EPA) and other agencies assign these numbers. Keep track of EPA numbers if there are problems or recalls.
- **Signal Word.** The registration process determines how toxic each pesticide is. Standard signal words must be used on the label:

Category	Signal Word
High toxicity	DANGER
Moderately toxic	WARNING

Low toxicity	CAUTION
Relatively non-toxic	NONE

- **Precautionary statements.** These describe the hazards associated with the chemical. They tell why the pesticide is hazardous. They list adverse effects. They state what PPE must be worn.
- **Statement of practical treatment.** This tells what to do in case of accidental exposure.
- **Statement of use classification.** The EPA classifies pesticides as either General-Use or Restricted-Use. Restricted-use pesticides can harm people, animals, or the environment.
- **Directions for use.** The directions tell how to apply the pesticide. They include how much to use, where to use it, and when to apply it. They also include the preharvest interval for all crops whenever appropriate.
- **Misuse statement.** This tells users to apply pesticides according to label directions.
- **Re-Entry Interval (REI) statement.** Sometimes, a certain amount of time must pass before a person can re-enter an area treated with a pesticide. This is the REI. The REI is included on the label or in state regulations.
- **Storage and disposal directions.** Improper storage can cause some pesticides to lose their effectiveness. It can also cause an explosion or fire. The label contains directions for proper storage and disposal.
- **Warranty.** The label informs you of your rights as a purchaser. It also limits the manufacturer's liability. The Safety Data Sheet (SDS) also contains information on the pesticide.

Review These Important Points

- Always read the labels before applying pesticides.
- Know what the warnings are and what they mean.
- Signal words identify the toxicity level. They represent relative risk.
- Know the signs of exposure before opening a container. Watch for those signs while working with the pesticide.
- Know the recommended response to accidental exposure before working with or around pesticides.

Topic:		
Instructor:	Location:	
Printed Name	**Signature**	**Date**

Topic: Repetitive Motion

Repetitive motion injuries occur when some action, usually involving bending or twisting, is done repeatedly. It can also be called cumulative trauma disorder or CTD. Pain or other warning signs may develop slowly. Many areas can be affected but the most common are fingers, hands, wrists, elbows, arms, shoulders, back, and neck.

If pain occurs in any area, do not ignore it. The pain will not go away. Instead, it will get worse. The injury will become more severe as time passes.

Repetitive Motion That Can Lead to Injuries

- Repetitive action of the hand or arm
- Bending at the wrist
- Grasping or pinching objects
- Frequently raising the arm and/or the shoulder
- Applying force with the hand or arm
- Examples
  - Pruning
  - Potting plants
  - Packing plants into boxes
  - Moving rolls of sod
  - Sweeping floors

Symptoms of an Injury

- Waking due to pain
- Numbness
- Tingling
- Swelling or tenderness
- Continuous aches
- Loss of strength
- Loss of joint movement
- Crackling
- Decreased coordination

Prevention

Prevention means working and playing smart. To eliminate repetitive motion injuries, try to adapt work activities. Plan how to use or move equipment so that the same motions are not repeated over and over. Be aware of repetitive motion used on and off the job. Repetitive motion trauma is most likely to occur after applying pressure or doing the same motion over and over. If pain occurs in spite of prevention, contact your doctor for an evaluation. Receiving an early evaluation and treatment is important.

Treatment

Your doctor may prescribe medication to help reduce inflammation and pain. Regular follow up visits with your doctor should be scheduled to check your progress. For more serious cases you may be referred to an occupational therapist.

In most cases the doctor will remove a person from the situation that is causing the injury. Time away from the situation, followed by a gradual return to an improved work situation, will be suggested by the doctor. Strengthening hand and arm muscles with exercise may be another suggestion. An improved work situation could be accomplished by simply changing motions so the same motion isn't continuously repeated. Including short rest breaks into your daily routine may also help.

Consider These Tips

- Avoid repeating the same motion for a long period of time.
- Work in a comfortable position.
- Force can cause injury to nerves, muscles, and tendons.
- Get plenty of rest.

Review These Important Points

- Work smart before using tools and equipment.
- Be aware of the repetitive motions included in your work.
- If pain or numbness occurs, see a doctor.
- Change work habits to change the repetitive motion.

Topic:		
Instructor:	Location:	

Printed Name	Signature	Date

Topic: Rollovers and Rollover Protective Structures (ROPS)

Tractor rollovers account for 50 percent of tractor-related deaths in the United States. Distracted operators, speed, and rough or uneven ground are leading causes of tractor rollovers. ROPS do not prevent rollovers, but they are 99.9 percent effective in preventing death or serious injury.

The Occupational Safety and Health Administration (OSHA) requires ROPS and seat belts to be installed on all tractors over 20 HP operated by employees.

Rollover Protective Structures (ROPS)

Rollover protective structures (ROPS) became available in the mid 1960s. ROPS were not available for all new tractors until the mid-1970s. However, ROPS were not standard equipment on new tractors until 1985. Many tractors without ROPS are still in use. They contribute to the fatality rate because they are not ROPS and seat-belt equipped. Use of ROPS and seat belts are 99.9 percent effective in preventing deaths due to tractor overturns.

There are three types of rollover protective structures:

- **Rollover protective frame.** Either two or four post frames are securely mounted to the main body of the tractor. Use the provided seat belt to keep the operator within the protected area.
- **Folding ROPS.** The top portion of the ROPS folds down so less overhead clearance is needed. This allows access to low-clearance areas like orchards or low overhead doors.
- **Rollover protective enclosure.** A rollover protective enclosure utilizes the protective frame but totally encloses the frame with metal and glass.

Seatbelts are provided and must be used to contain the operator within the protected area. In addition, a cab enclosure gives protection from weather, dust, chemicals, noise, and vibration.

Enclosures on older tractors were designed for operator comfort, not for rollover protection. They are not considered ROPS. ROPS must meet regulations and standards that certify that they provide adequate protection in a tractor rollover. To find out if a frame or enclosure is certified, look for a certification label, contact the manufacturer, or check for the presence of a manufacturer installed seat belt.

For tractors not equipped with a ROPS, check with the manufacturer or dealer for the availability of ROPS retrofit kits. If they are available, the tractor should be retrofitted. If kits are not available, the tractor should not be operated. Install and use seat belts on tractors with ROPS. Seat belts ensure that the operator stays within the zone of protection offered by the ROPS during a mishap. Seat belts should not be used on tractors without ROPS.

Reducing the Risk of a Side Rollover

- Set the wheels as far apart as possible.
- Lock the brake pedals together before high-speed road travel.
- Match speed to operating conditions and loads. Do not let the front wheels bounce.
- Slow down before turning.
- Use engine braking when going downhill.
- Avoid crossing steep slopes. Watch for depressions on the downhill side and bumps on the uphill side. Turn downhill, not uphill, if stability becomes a problem.
- Stay 10 feet or more away from ditches and steep slopes. Slow down to maintain control.
- Stay 10 feet or more from a riverbank. The bank may be steep. Slow down to maintain control.
- Keep front-end loader buckets as low as possible when moving.
- If the right front tire goes off the road into the ditch, turn downward or hold steady and slowly recover. Do not attempt to turn sharply back onto the roadway.

Reducing the Risk for Rear Overturn

- Always hitch loads at the drawbar.
- Use front weights to increase tractor stability.
- Start forward motion slowly and change speed gradually.
- If possible, avoid backing downhill.
- Drive around ditches.
- Back out or be towed out of ditches or mud.

Review These Important Points

- Install and use seat belts on tractors with ROPS.
- ROPS do not prevent rollovers from occurring.
- Most rollovers involve tractor speed, operator error, or unsafe driving conditions.
- Follow safety steps to prevent rollovers.

Topic:		
Instructor:	Location:	
Printed Name	**Signature**	**Date**

Topic: Rotary Lawn and Brush Mower Safety

Knowing the capabilities of the mower allows for the use of the right mower for the job. The operator's manual will help determine if the mower is designed for the job. Keep bystanders away from:

- Mowing/tractor controls.
- Mowing blade.
- Throwing distance and direction for that blade.

Never allow riders on the equipment.

Remove all litter and debris from the area to be mowed. Stones, tin cans, and wire can be deadly when thrown by a mower blade. Be alert for holes and ditches; these hazards may cause the driver to lose control of the mower.

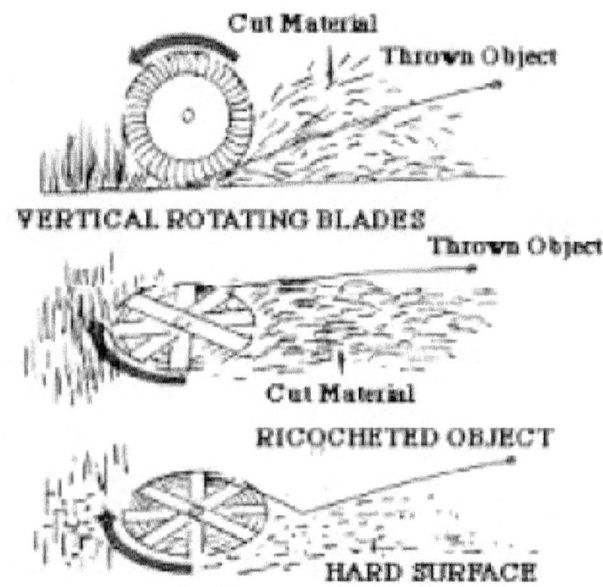

When using a tractor equipped with a rollover protective structure (ROPS), wear a seat belt. Wear tight and belted clothing that won't get tangled in moving parts. Wear protective equipment for eyes, hair, hands, hearing, and head.

Before dismounting from the tractor, always disengage the power-take-off (PTO), turn off the engine, and set the brakes. When approaching the mower, make sure that the blades are not rotating. Be aware that the blades will continue to rotate for a while after the power has been shut off.

Be cautious while making turns. If the rear tractor wheel of a pull-type mower catches the mower frame, it could throw the operator. The three-point hitch-mounted mower can swing outward when turning. Adding front wheel weights for balance and control and a wide setting for the rear tires enhances tractor stability and reduces the chance of a tractor overturn. Do not operate on steep slopes. Operate at a safe speed.

Hazard risks increase when equipment is not well maintained. Know the proper maintenance procedures. Check machinery for loose parts and blade sharpness. Replace blades that are too dull to sharpen. Rotary mowers are equipped with runners and safety guards. To avoid excessive wear on the runners, keep the mower just high enough to avoid riding on the runner shoes.

Keep all guards in place and well maintained. The PTO must be shielded. Use chain or belt guards to reduce the possibility of objects being thrown from under the mower

Manufacturers recommend that children not be allowed to operate a tractor equipped with a rotary mower because of the danger involved. Young workers may be able to operate a sit-down mower of less than 20 horsepower — but only on level ground and with supervision. Under federal child labor regulations, 14- and 15-yearolds may not operate power-driven machinery like rotary lawn and brush mowers.

Safety Tips

- Keep all guards in place.
- Drive cautiously and know the area.
- Always read the owner's/operator's manual.
- Keep others away from the area being mowed.
- No riders — driver only.
- Know the child labor laws.
- Wear a seat belt when the tractor is equipped with ROPS.

Review These Important Points

- Know the capabilities of the mower.
- Check for debris, holes, and obstacles prior to mowing.
- Add tractor weights and wider tires if needed.
- Know and follow maintenance procedures.
- Keep all guards in place at all times.
- Know the law when hiring youth to drive mowers.

Topic:		
Instructor:	Location:	

Printed Name	Signature	Date

Topic: Safe Use of Flammable Liquids

Many useful liquids are flammable — they can cause a fire. To prevent fires, all flammable liquids must be clearly labeled. Liquids and rags must be stored in the right container. Sparks and smoking must be avoided. You must dispose of spilled liquids or leftovers safely.

Storing Flammable Liquids

Flammables should be stored in a self-closing safety can. Flammables stored in open containers can vaporize. Vapors can ignite or explode if a lighted match or spark is present.

Store gasoline only in a red container. Remember it will ignite if it comes into contact with a hot surface. So, allow any engine to cool before refueling.

Storing Liquid-Soaked Rags

Store liquid-soaked rags in a metal container with a tight-fitting lid. This keeps oxygen away, reducing the chance of a fire. When exposed to air, some rags can produce enough heat to ignite spontaneously. Keep all flammables in a specific storage cabinet, well marked with warning signs.

Fire Control

Control all ignition sources around flammables. Enforce the **No Smoking Rule** around flammable liquids. Keep sparking tools away from flammables. Use non-sparking electrical equipment around flammables. There **must** be a fire extinguisher within 75 feet of all bulk transfer stations.

Some materials can ignite from the small energy in a static spark. So, ground and bond all bulk containers during dispensing and pouring. There must be a conductive connection between the receiving container, dispensing container, and a specially installed ground pipe. When drawing liquids from a bulk tank to a portable container, there should be a solid connection between the tank and the container. Self-closing valves on dispensing and pouring containers will minimize spills. Drums stored outdoors in warm weather may require pressure relief venting caps.

Clean Up and Disposal

You might spill flammable liquids and other chemicals — solvents, pesticides, nitrate fertilizers, or bleach. Or, you may have leftovers. Spills or leftovers become chemical hazardous waste. Clean up and dispose of Hazardous waste according to local, state, and federal regulations. Chemical hazardous waste disposal is expensive.

Leftovers can often be used or applied elsewhere. But you must take care to use them before they expire.

Identification

Identify flammable liquid containers by a red diamond-shaped label with black lettering.

Review These Important Points

- Never store flammables in open or unapproved containers.
- Store flammables in a special storage cabinet that is well marked with warning signs for everyone to see.
- Control all ignition sources around flammable liquids.
- Never smoke around flammable liquids.
- Ground and bond bulk containers because some materials can be ignited by the minimal energy in a static spark.

Topic:		
Instructor:	Location:	

Printed Name	**Signature**	**Date**

Topic: Safe Use of Hand-Held Tools

Wrenches, hammers, pliers. Pruning saws and tools. Crowbars, screwdrivers. Hand hooks, files, and scrapers. Each of these tools might be in your toolbox, and each one needs to be used safely, for the right job.

General Safety Tips

- Personal Protection Equipment can help prevent injuries.
- Stop working if safety glasses become fogged. Clean glasses until lenses are clear.
- Don't carry sharp or pointed tools in your pocket unless the tool is in a sheath.
- Even better, carry all hand tools in a toolbox or tool belt.

Wrenches

Use the appropriate size and type of wrench for the nut. Is the nut an English or a metric size? Can a closed-end wrench (also called a box-end wrench) be used for a good fit, or is an open-end wrench necessary to reach the nut? Socket wrenches and ratchets allow turning a nut in a tight location. An adjustable wrench must be used properly; make sure the adjustable jaw faces the operator. Wrenches are manufactured in many sizes with a leverage length appropriate to the size nut to be moved. It is unsafe to use a length of pipe to gain more leverage. Pipe wrenches and locking pliers are not appropriate for use on nuts because a corner of the nut may be broken.

Hammers

Use the right type of hammer for the specific job. Never strike hardened steel surfaces with a steel hammer. Use a soft metal hammer or one with a plastic, wood, or rawhide head when striking steel surfaces to align or loosen them. Always wear safety glasses to protect your eyes from small pieces of metal that may fly off the hammer or the object being hit. Inspect all hammers carefully, including large sledgehammers, before use to be sure the head is tight and undamaged. Replace damaged handles; make sure the hammer fits the head properly. Wedge the handle securely in the head and make sure it is free of splinters and cracks.

Pliers

Never substitute pliers for another tool such as a wrench to complete the task. It may cause the bolt heads to become chewed. Pliers cannot grip nuts and bolts securely and will slip. If working with electricity, use hand insulated grips. Make sure the protective coverings are free from cracks or holes. Use a vise when cutting wire with the pliers. Hold the open end of the wire with your free hand, foot, or other means to prevent the cutoff piece from flying through the air.

Screwdrivers

- Don't use a screwdriver with wet or greasy hands.
- Don't use a screwdriver to test a battery charge.
- Don't use a screwdriver to chisel or pry or punch.
- Pick a screwdriver with the right size and type of head for the screw.
- Make a starting hole for the screw with a nail or a drill.
- Don't hold the work piece against your body. Steady it on a sturdy flat surface.
- Keep your fingers away from the blade while you're using a screwdriver.
- Don't use pliers or a hammer to force the screwdriver.
- For electrical work, use a screwdriver with a blue handle. It is insulated!

Pruning Equipment

Use caution when using lopping shears, hand shears, pruning or bow saws, and related pruning tools. Accidents can cause amputated fingers, serious cuts, and significant blood loss.

In particular, use caution when pruning overhead. Limbs or the pruning tool can fall on you, and power lines are a real danger. Contact with a power line can electrocute you.

When storing pruning tools, always keep them locked up in the sheaths provided or in other protective housing units to avoid injury to handlers.

Saws
- Don't use any saw with a dull blade.
- Some saws have adjustable blades — hacksaw, coping saw, keyhole saw, or bow saw. Make sure the blade is taut before using it.
- Keep the saw under control. At the end of the stroke, let up on downward pressure.
- Hold the work piece firmly against your work surface.
- Keep fingers and hands away from the blade while sawing.
- Oil the blade after you use a saw.
- Don't carry a saw by the blade.

Chisels
- Always use a sharp chisel — not one with a dull cutting blade.
- If the head of the handle is mushroomed, do not use it.
- If possible, hold a chisel with a holder, not your hand.
- Always chisel away from your body.
- Clamp any small work piece in a vise. Chisel toward the stationary jaw.

Other Tools
- Always use each tool for the specific job intended.
- Crowbars should be used only for jobs that require prying.
- Files must be cleaned with a file card after use. Do not strike the file against another piece of metal.
- Hand hooks must be kept sharp to prevent slipping when in use. They should be stored with the point in cork to reduce accidents.
- Scrapers must be kept in good, sharp condition for best results.

Review These Important Points
- Use the right tool for the job.
- Always wear safety glasses/goggles to prevent serious eye damage.
- It is unsafe to add more leverage to any tool by use of an extension.
- Use the shop vise when the job requires.

Topic:		
Instructor:	Location:	
Printed Name	**Signature**	**Date**

Topic: Safe Use of the Power-Take-Off (PTO)

Most power shafts can be extended from the power source to another piece of equipment. This connection is called a power-take-off (PTO). The power source is whatever the PTO is connected to — a tractor, an all-terrain vehicle (ATV), lawnmower, or other equipment.

Power shafts are usually constructed with a square shaft inserted into a housing or casing. It is important that at least 5-1/2 inches of the sliding shaft remain in the housing when the power shaft is connected to the power source. This reduces the possibility of the shafts separating while the equipment is in motion. If the shaft splits, the portion of the shaft connected to the power source is free to whirl at high speeds, endangering the worker and equipment.

People cannot react fast enough to pull away from a spinning shaft, and most clothing is strong enough to pull a person into the spinning shaft. Very serious injury and, more frequently, death is the end result of these accidents.

PTO Safety Guidelines

Before you start the power source, **be sure the PTO is disengaged.** If the PTO is already engaged when you start the power source, the equipment powered by the PTO will begin to operate.

Use extreme caution when operating equipment with a separable PTO shaft. Never hook 540-rpm (revolutions per minute) equipment to a 1,000-rpm PTO or vice versa.

If the shaft does separate, **disengage the PTO immediately and stop the power unit.**

Keep **safety shields** securely fastened on the equipment. Periodic inspections and maintenance of the shields/guards may be necessary. Safe operation of the PTO is not possible without these shields in place. A sudden slip or fall could throw a worker directly onto the unshielded rotation shaft. Also, those who are unfamiliar with the equipment may not recognize the danger of the power shaft.

Wear snug-fitting clothes when working around power shafts. Loose clothing can catch in or be wrapped around the power shaft. Do not step over an operating PTO. A sudden slip or a loose shoestring could cause the worker to become entangled in the PTO shaft. Long hair may also become entangled in a PTO shaft. Hair should be pulled back out of the way and secured. Also avoid any type of jewelry that could become entangled, causing dismemberment or bodily injury.

Review These Important Points

- Keep all PTO guards and shields in place, even when the PTO is not operating.
- Always disconnect the PTO when not in use.
- Never engage the PTO while the machine engine is shut off.
- Keep hands, feet, clothing, and long hair away from the PTO.
- Never operate PTO shafts at extreme angles.
- Be sure that the PTO spinner shields rotate freely at all times.
- Always disengage all power and shut off equipment before servicing.

Topic:		
Instructor:	Location:	

Printed Name	Signature	Date

Topic: Safe Use of Tractors and Self-Propelled Equipment

Many workers in the green industry use tractors on the job. In addition, workers might use other self-propelled equipment:

- Traveling or watering booms
- Conveyors
- Shipping carts
- Bench transports
- Golf carts
- Utility vehicles

General Safety Guidelines

Read and follow the operator's safety manual. Keep safety signs in good repair. Replace them as needed. When a part is replaced, transfer the safety equipment to the new part. Replacement safety signs can be bought from a dealer.

Describe how to operate all controls on the equipment. Keep the equipment in good working condition. Do not modify equipment. Do not modify the safety devices. Unauthorized modification can impair the operation and safety of the equipment.

Tractors are powerful machines. They require careful attention to operate and service. New tractors are equipped with safety devices. These devices provide a reasonable amount of protection. Practice good safety habits. Be aware of hazardous situations.

Safe Operation of Equipment

- Safe operation depends on alert and efficient handling. Most accidents occur when the driver is tired or not alert.
- Only trained workers should operate tractors and self-propelled equipment.
- Wear safety glasses to prevent eye damage due to flying debris. Wear snug-fitting clothing. This lessens the chance of clothing catching on a moving part.
- Do not ride double unless a seat is provided.
- Before you start, check the work area for debris, obstacles, ditches, and holes. They could cause the tractor to overturn.
- Be aware of weather conditions. Control is more difficult in mud, snow, or ice.
- The tractor should be equipped with a rollover protective structure (ROPS). This device will protect the driver in case of an overturn. Fasten the seat belt only if there is a ROPS.
- A first aid kit should be on or near all major equipment.

Machines with mounted equipment need adequate ballast for stability. Hitch loads to the draw bar to prevent turning over backwards when pulling. To avoid overturns, back out of deep ditches, up slopes, and out of mud holes. Slow down and begin turning the wheels before applying the brake. This will help avoid overturns, skidding, and bouncing. Sitting down with the seat belt fastened is always encouraged. It is mandatory when traveling over rough terrain. It lessens the chance of the driver being thrown from the machine.

Review These Important Points

- Stay alert. Recognize and follow safety procedures.
- No riders (except during the training session).
- First aid should be readily available.
- Follow recommended guidelines in difficult terrain and weather conditions.
- Read and follow the operator's manual.

Topic:

Instructor: Location:

Printed Name	Signature	Date

Topic: Safely Starting and Stopping a Tractor

Tractors are common and look easy to operate. However, accidents can happen if safety is not observed.

Mounting the Tractor

Before mounting the tractor, make sure guards and shields are in place and in good working condition. Use provided handrails for mounting and dismounting. Adjust the operator's seat for fit and easy access to controls.

Starting the Tractor

Before starting the engine remember to:

- Place the gearshift lever in Neutral or Park.
- Place all hydraulic controls in neutral.
- Disengage the power-take-off (PTO).
- Apply the brakes.
- Depress the clutch pedal.

Tractors will start in gear if normal starting circuitry is bypassed. Start the engine from the operator's seat with the transmission in park. Do not start the engine by shorting across starter terminals. Never start the engine while you are standing on the ground. If jumper cables are needed to start the engine, make sure polarity is correct. Reversed polarity will damage the electrical system. Always connect the positive cable first and then the negative cable. Escaping gas can cause an explosion, so position the ground connection away from the battery. This will help keep sparks away from the battery. Follow the instructions in the tractor operator's manual. Always wear eye protection when working around batteries.

Stopping the Tractor

Stopping the tractor safely involves more than just applying the brakes and turning off the engine. To avoid accidents:

- Lock the brake pedals together when driving.
- Apply the brakes evenly.
- Disengage the PTO.
- Lower all hydraulically powered equipment to the ground.
- Put the gearshift lever in Park or Neutral and set the brakes.
- Turn the ignition key off and remove it to prevent tampering or accidental starting.

Additional Safety Hints

- Keep a copy of the operator's manual on the tractor or close by.
- To prevent falls, keep the operator station free of oil, grease, mud, and tools.
- Keep trash away from the exhaust system to prevent a fire.
- Keep tires properly inflated.
- Maintain control lights and gauges.
- Ventilate to avoid asphyxiation when operating tractors indoors.

Review These Important Points

- No riders (except for specific training purposes).
- Never start the engine by shorting across starter terminals.
- When jump-starting an engine, avoid sparks around the battery and wear eye protection.
- Always apply brakes evenly and disengage the PTO before stopping the tractor.
- Lock the brake pedals together when driving.

Topic:		
Instructor:	Location:	

Printed Name	Signature	Date

Topic: Skin Irritations Caused by Plants

Many plants can cause skin irritations in humans. Some workers may be more sensitive to certain plants than other workers. Generally, there are five categories — poison plants, allergenic plants (and plant parts), skin irritant plants, stinging plants, and thorn plants.

- **Poison plants** include poison ivy, poison oak, and poison sumac. They all contain a toxin called urishiol. This toxin is present in the sap of the plant. Touching this type of plant can cause skin rashes and blisters.
- **Allergenic plants** (and plant parts) include, among others, orchids, tulip bulbs, chrysanthemums, and dahlias. They cause allergic reactions in some people. The pollen in these plants can cause hay fever or asthma.
- **Skin irritant plants** include, among others, poinsettias, penciltrees, daffodils, hyacinths, and buttercups. These plants can cause skin irritations.
- **Stinging plants** have nettles. Touching a nettle can cause a toxic reaction. However, the reaction does not last long and has no lasting effect.
- **Thorn plants** include, among others, roses, blackberry and raspberry bushes, and black locust and honey locust trees. Infection can result from an embedded thorn. A scratch can also cause an infection especially if dirt gets into the scratch.

How to Avoid Skin Irritations

- If you handle plants, wear gloves, a long-sleeve shirt, and long pants. Wear work shoes or boots. Do not wear open-toed shoes or sandals.
- Never burn plants that may be toxic. Toxins can be present in the smoke.
- Learn what problem plants grow in your area and how to identify them.
- If you touch a poisonous plant, obtain treatment immediately.
- Never eat wild berries or plant leaves.
- After handling plants, always wash your hands and other exposed skin before eating, drinking, smoking, or going to the bathroom.
- Wash your clothes separately in hot water. Clean your shoes with rubbing alcohol and water.
- If you have a severe reaction to a plant, such as a rash or blisters, see a doctor.

Review These Important Points

- Learn to recognize what problem plants look like, such as dahlias, hyacinths, daffodils, and blackberry bushes.
- Wear proper clothing to lessen the chance of plants touching your skin.
- Always wash your clothing separately in hot water.
- Never eat wild berries or plant leaves.
- Never burn plants that may be toxic. Toxins can be present in the smoke.
- Obtain treatment immediately if you develop a rash or blisters.

Printed Name	Signature	Date
Topic:		
Instructor:	Location:	

Topic:

Instructor: Location:

Printed Name	Signature	Date

Topic: Small-Engine Machine Safety

You may use small engine machines such as push mowers, weed trimmers, and leaf blowers. You should know how to operate and maintain them in a safe manner. If possible, read the operator's manual. It will contain detailed information on the safe operation and maintenance of the machine. If your employer does not have a manual, ask if one can be ordered from the manufacturer.

Small Engine Safety

- Always check the oil level before starting the engine. Add oil if necessary. Always use the type of oil that is recommended in the operator's manual.
- If the engine requires a mixture of oil and gasoline, be sure to use the proper ratio. Refer to the operator's manual for the correct mixture.
- Never fill the gasoline tank if the engine is hot. Allow it to cool down for several minutes before refueling. Clean up any spilled gasoline before starting the engine.
- Do not smoke while filling the gas tank or operating the machine.
- Store gasoline in an approved, properly labeled container. Use only gasoline approved for the engine.
- Never start the engine in an enclosed space. Always start it in a well-ventilated area. Carbon monoxide or fumes can be dangerous in an enclosed space.
- Never touch the engine muffler while it is hot. The engine muffler can get extremely hot. And it stays hot for some time after the engine is shut off. You could be seriously burned should you accidentally touch it.
- Never perform any kind of adjustment while the engine is running.
- Always disconnect the spark plug before performing maintenance and safety checks on small-engine machines.
- When the machine is not in use, disconnect the spark plug. This safety procedure will lessen the possibility of the machine accidentally starting.
- Allow the machine to cool off before storing in an enclosed space.

General Safety Tips

- Always wear personal protection clothing such as safety goggles with shields, earmuffs or earplugs, leather or cotton gloves, long pants, and rubber-soled work boots or shoes. Do not wear tennis shoes, sandals, or open-toed shoes.
- Remove any loose debris (trash, tree limbs, rocks, etc.) before you start.
- Make sure the area where you will be working is clear of all other workers or bystanders, especially small children and pets. Check the operator's manual for proper clearance of flying debris.
- Never operate a machine while under the influence of alcohol, drugs, or medication.
- Never remove any safety guards or shields. They are there for your protection.

Push Mower Safety

- Start the mower from a firm stance with both feet in a safe position.
- If the mower has a self-propelled mechanism, make sure it is disengaged before you start the engine. If the self-propelled mechanism is in gear, the mower will start to move once the engine has started.
- Never use an electric mower in wet grass. You could receive an electrical shock.
- Never perform any kind of adjustment while the mower is running. For example, if you want to change the height of the wheels, first turn the engine off and disconnect the spark plug. Then reposition the wheels.
- Always push the mower in a forward direction. Never pull the mower toward you. If you slip, your foot could go under the mower deck resulting in a serious injury.

- If the mower deck should become clogged with grass, stop the mower and turn the engine off before clearing the clog. Never touch any part of the mower while operating it except for the handles and throttles.
- If the mower has an attached grass catcher, stop the engine before detaching the grass catcher. Do not let the grass catcher become too full. A full or over-full catcher adds wear and tear on the engine, and the mower does not cut as well.
- Perform a safety check before and after each time you use the mower. Check and tighten all loose nuts, bolts, and screws. If the mower has a drive belt, check for frayed or worn sections. Replace the belt if necessary.
- Clean the mower after each use, including the underside of the mower deck. Clean the grass catcher, if the mower has one.

Weed Trimmer Safety and Operator Tips
- Keep your hands, face, and feet away from any moving parts. Do not touch the trimmer string while it is rotating.
- If the trimmer should become entangled, stop the engine immediately. Then untangle the trimmer line. Check for damage before restarting the engine.
- Do not overreach. Always be properly balanced. Be alert if the area you are trimming is wet or on a slope.
- Perform a safety check before and after each time you use the trimmer. Check and tighten all loose nuts, bolts, and screws.
- Clean the trimmer after each use.

Leaf Blower Safety and Operator Tips
- Keep your hands, face, and feet away from any moving parts.
- If your working area is dusty, wear a dust mask.
- Do not overreach. Always be properly balanced. Be alert if the area you are trimming is wet or on a slope. Use caution while working on steps.
- Never operate an electric blower if the area is wet.
- Make sure the air intake is always free of debris.
- Perform a safety check before and after each time you use the blower. Check and tighten all loose nuts, bolts, and screws.
- Clean the blower after each use.

Review These Important Points
- Always wear proper clothing and eye and ear protection while operating small machines.
- Make sure the area is clear of other people where you will be working.
- Always keep all safety shields in place.
- Never touch moving parts.
- Never operate a machine while under the influence of alcohol, drugs, or medication.
- Perform a safety and maintenance check before and after each time you use the machine.
- Clean the machine after each use.

Topic:		
Instructor:	Location:	
Printed Name	**Signature**	**Date**

Topic: Spider Bites

Many people are afraid of spiders, but the majority of spiders are harmless to humans. In fact, most spiders are beneficial predators that reduce pest populations such as flies, crickets, and mites in and around yards, gardens, and crops. Spiders normally will not attempt to bite unless accidentally trapped against the skin or grasped. However, some actively guard their egg sacs or young. Most spiders prefer warmer climates and dark, dry places where flies are plentiful.

Only a few spiders like the black widow spider and the brown recluse are dangerous to workers. The black widow is known for the red hourglass marking on its underside. Black widow spider webs are usually built in woodpiles, rubble piles, under stones, in hollow stumps, and in rodent burrows.

Brown recluse spiders are very secretive. They can often be found under rocks, in crevices, or inside boxes or containers. Brown recluses are brown in color. They have three pairs of eyes, one pair in the middle and another pair toward each side of their head. They may have a pattern like a violin on their underside — but not always.

Symptoms of Spider Bites

Spider bites can have different symptoms. Most are very mild and need not cause concern:

- Painless bite, not even noticed.
- Slight feeling, like a pinprick, when bitten.
- Slight swelling at the site.

However, other symptoms are more serious:

- Sharp, stinging sensation when bitten.
- Significant swelling at the site.
- Breathing problems.
- Dizziness, with some nausea.
- Swelling of the lips or throat.
- Faintness.
- Confusion.
- Rapid heartbeat.
- Hives.

These serious symptoms call for medical attention — fast. They may indicate a black widow or brown recluse bite, or they may indicate that the worker is allergic to spider bites in general. A cloth dampened with cold water or filled with ice may be applied to the bite while awaiting help.

Preventing Spider Bites

- Shake out clothing and shoes before getting dressed.
- Check before working near vines, brush, overgrown grass, and wooded habitats.
- Wear gloves when handling firewood, lumber, and rocks.
- Install yellow or sodium vapor light bulbs outdoors since these attract fewer insects for spiders to feed upon.
- Do not stack wood against a building.
- Remove heavy vegetation and leaf litter around building foundations.

Review These Important Points

- Black widow spider webs are usually built in woodpiles, rubble piles, under stones, in hollow stumps, and in rodent burrows.
- Install yellow or sodium vapor light bulbs outdoors since these attract fewer insects for spiders to feed upon.
- Check before working near vines, brush, overgrown grass, and wooded habitats.

Topic:		
Instructor:	Location:	
Printed Name	**Signature**	**Date**

Topic: Stress Management

Green industry service businesses are stressful occupations. For example, seasonal workloads can vary greatly. Seasonal demands lead to long work hours, and those long hours can be a source of stress. Working outdoors in the weather can also add stress. Heat, cold, humidity, precipitation, and winds can all lead to stress. Work delays caused by bad weather can add more stress, especially during peak seasonal workloads.

It is important to know how to manage stress levels and to reduce the effects of unwanted stress. One way to manage stress is to talk to other people. This support might come from family, church members, friends, or other workers. There are also several organized self-help groups that offer emotional support and practical help. Consult a family doctor, mental health professional, or religious leader for additional help.

Stress Can Be Reduced by Making Lifestyle Changes

- Keep a positive attitude.
- Accept that stress is a part of life.
- Clearly define home and work responsibilities.
- Manage time.
- Set realistic goals.
- Learn to relax. Employees who take mid-morning and afternoon breaks will be able to get more accomplished.
- Eat well-balanced meals.
- Develop an exercise program.

Eat an adequate and nutritious breakfast each day. A nutritious breakfast should include protein plus fresh fruit and vegetables. Hunger can make people less able to cope with stress. High blood pressure and cholesterol levels increase the chances of a stroke and heart attack. Caffeine (coffee, tea, soft drinks, and some drugs) stimulates the nervous system and can cause nervousness and tension. If you tend to be tense or nervous, reduce your consumption of caffeine. Alcohol and drugs can be addictive and may reduce your ability to cope with stress. A basic exercise program, in addition to daily work, is likely to lessen stress. Exercise will produce a healthier heart, lungs, and arteries and will elevate your mood and encourage a healthy self-concept. Have a complete medical exam before beginning an exercise program.

Finally, know the warning signs of stress-related problems and seek help.

Early Warning Signs of Stress-Related Problems

- Moodiness
- Withdrawing from responsibility
- Trouble falling asleep
- Poor emotional control
- Severe feelings of helplessness and dependency
- Chronic fatigue and susceptibility to illness
- Marked change in appetite or sex drive

If any of these problems persist, consult a doctor.

Review These Important Points

- Stress can be managed.
- Seek help when a problem is discovered.
- A positive attitude makes a difference.
- Eat a well-balanced diet.

Topic:		
Instructor:	Location:	
Printed Name	**Signature**	**Date**

Topic: Struck-By Accidents

Struck-by accidents are those where an object hits the worker. Overhead storage shelves, racks, hangers, aisles, passageways, and doors can be a source of danger. Careless work habits can make hazards worse. Struck-by accidents can also occur during tree trimming, pruning, and felling. The tree or tree limbs can fall and strike workers on the ground or in the tree. Bent limbs can also strike workers when the limb is released and springs back.

Potential Struck-By Accident Hazards

- Tools or loose parts left on window ledges, shelves, cranes, or working platforms.
- Objects leaning against walls, racks, posts, or equipment.
- Inadequate guarding on belts or no side barriers on conveyors traveling from one level to another.
- Unmarked low beams or pipes.
- No screen guard on equipment or poor or incomplete screening to guard against objects flying off the equipment.
- Weak overhead supports or poor stacking of materials.

Eliminate Hazards

- Don't leave tools or loose parts on window ledges, shelves, cranes, or working platforms. If you see any left loose, report them or remove them.
- Leave guards or screens in place on equipment as it was manufactured.
- Mark low beams, pipes, and ceilings with proper *Low Clearance – Caution* signs.
- Stack and store objects properly.
- If there is a potential danger from overhead hazards, wear an approved hard hat or bump hat.
- Use falling object protective structures (FOPS) on equipment.
- Be alert and report all hazards.

Aisles and Doors

- Keep aisles and passageways clear and well marked.
- Allow safe aisle and door clearance to prevent getting caught or knocking down material.
- If a door swings out into a hallway, mark the door swing on the floor.
- Never stand in front of a windowless, swinging door.
- Before working near a door, post a warning sign or prop the door open. This is especially important if working from a ladder.
- Do not push a door open rapidly or forcefully. Someone may be on the other side.
- When approaching double doors, follow signs indicating which door to use.

Pay Attention

- Watch where you are going.
- Do not get distracted by conversations.
- Approach a corner or intersection from the center of the hall. Plan to walk to the right, reducing the chance of oncoming collisions.

Review These Important Points

- Wear a hard hat or bump hat if necessary for the job.
- Watch for falling objects or items that block aisles.
- Keep all screens and guards in place.
- Use safe storage and handling procedures.

Topic:		
Instructor:	Location:	
Printed Name	**Signature**	**Date**

Topic: Sun Exposure

Workers in the green industry work long hours, often outside in the sun. During peak season, workers can spend even more hours exposed to the sun. However, too much exposure to the sun can cause skin cancer. About 800,000 new skin cancer cases are diagnosed each year. Proper personal protection must be used to limit skin exposure.

Sun exposure is a key factor in the development of skin cancers. Basal cell and squamous cell skin cancer risk is linked with cumulative sun exposure. Malignant melanoma risk is linked with cumulative sun exposure and the number of severe burns. Some people have greater risk of skin changes and skin cancer from sun exposure:

- People who burn easily, rarely tan, and have freckles.
- People who have a fair complexion.
- People with blonde or red hair.
- People with blue or gray eyes.

Watch for Skin Cancer

You should check any skin spot that spontaneously bleeds, changes color, or changes size. A self-exam guide can help you decide when you should see a doctor. The American Cancer Society has a good self-exam guide. Look for these physical signs:

- Asymmetrical spots.
- Irregular borders.
- Color variations.
- Diameters bigger than the end of a pencil eraser.

If you have any questions about the possibility of skin cancer, consult a doctor.

Skin Cancers

- **Basal cell** cancer look shiny. It usually can be cut away or treated topically. If diagnosed and treated early, it can be cured. It is more of a concern later in life.
- **Squamous cell** cancer looks rusty and warty. It usually can be cut away or treated topically. If it is diagnosed and treated early, it can be cured. It is more of a concern later in life.
- **Melanoma** looks like a dark mole. However, malignant melanoma can be dangerous, even fatal. Melanoma cases have been steadily rising. It affects people of all ages.

To Minimize the Risk of Skin Cancer

- Protective clothing acts as a barrier between the skin and the sun. So, wear long sleeves, long pants, high socks, and gloves. Tighter woven fabrics provide greater protection. Lighter colored clothing reflects heat better.
- Wear a wide brimmed hat, cap flap, or the flap on cap. A baseball cap offers the least protection. Baseball hats do not protect ear tips, temples, or the back of the neck.
- Use a sunscreen with a sun protection factor (SPF) of 15 or more while working outdoors. Reapply the sunscreen every two hours.
- Wear sunglasses to block ultraviolet (UV) rays and protect the eyes from sun exposure.
- While working outdoors in the sun, you can get dehydrated. Dehydration can be very serious. Drink one glass of water every 15 to 30 minutes.

Review These Important Points

- Skin cancers are the most common cancers experienced in the United States.
- The major cause of skin cancers is the amount of time a person is exposed to the sun.
- Wear protective clothing that serves as a barrier between the sun and the skin.

Topic:		
Instructor:	Location:	

Printed Name	Signature	Date

Topic: Thorn Bushes

Many bushes, shrubs, and scrub trees have thorns. Some examples are rose, multiflora rose, blackberry, and raspberry bushes. If you have to work near or with these plants, be aware that the thorns are sharp. Thorns can cause cuts, lacerations, and scratches to your skin.

How to Avoid Contact With Thorns

- Always wear gloves. Leather gloves are best.
- Wear a long-sleeve shirt and long pants. Clothing made of thicker cloth is better.
- Wear work shoes or boots. Do not wear sandals or open-toed shoes.
- If you are cutting bushes, wear eye protection and a safety hard hat.

If Cuts, Lacerations, or Scratches Occur

- Try not to get dirt into the scratch or wound. Dirt can cause an infection.
- Clean the wound with rubbing alcohol.
- Apply iodine or an anti-bacterial ointment.
- If the scratch is deep, apply a band-aid or bandage.
- If infection should occur, see a doctor.

Review These Important Points

- Be aware that thorns are sharp and can scratch or cut your skin.
- Always wear gloves when you handle thorn bushes.
- Clean cuts and scratches with rubbing alcohol and apply iodine or an anti-bacterial ointment.

Topic:		
Instructor:	Location:	
Printed Name	**Signature**	**Date**

Topic: Tick Bites

Working in landscaping, forestry, or brush clearing can be risky because of exposure to ticks. The most frequently encountered ticks are the American dog tick and the ground hog tick. They can be found on various mammals, including ground hogs, raccoons, dogs, and humans. Deer tick and western black-legged ticks are much smaller than common dog and cattle ticks.

When ticks feed on animals, they can acquire diseases including Lyme Disease and Rocky Mountain Spotted Fever. Then, ticks can pass the disease on to humans. Often, emergency help should be sought right away. Workers who are bitten should identify the tick to help doctors diagnose the trouble.

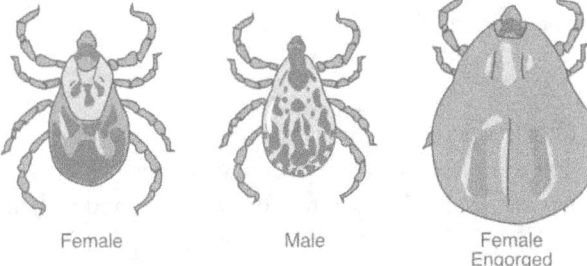

Female   Male   Female
                             Engorged

American Dog Ticks

Lyme Disease Symptoms	Rocky Mountain Spotted Fever Symptoms

• Bulls-eye rash
   o Looks like a bulls-eye, with a reddish outer ring and a pale center
   o Warm to the touch
   o Usually more than two inches in diameter
   o Occurs in 75 percent of those infected with Lyme disease.
• Fever
• Lymph node swelling
• Neck stiffness
• Generalized fatigue
• Headaches
• Migrating joint aches
• Muscle aches
	• Initial symptoms may include:
	   o Fever
	   o Nausea
	   o Vomiting
	   o Severe headache
	   o Muscle pain
	   o Lack of appetite
	• Later signs and symptoms include:
	   o Rash
	   o Abdominal pain
	   o Joint pain
	   o Diarrhea
	The three classic symptoms are fever, rash, and history of tick bite.

Preventing Tick Bites

- Stay out of brushy, overgrown grass, and wooded habitats, especially in spring and early summer.
- Remove leaves, tall grass, and brush from work areas. This will reduce tick, deer, and rodent habitat.
- Apply tick-toxic chemicals to work areas to help control the tick population.
- Wear light-colored clothing so ticks may be more easily seen and removed before attaching.
- Wear long-sleeve shirts. Tuck pant legs into socks or boots.
- Wear high boots or enclosed shoes that cover the entire foot.
- Wear a hat.
- Spray insect repellent on exposed skin, excluding the face.
- Shower and wash and dry clothes at a high temperature after outdoor exposure.
- Check your whole body for ticks, especially armpits, groin, and pubic areas.
- If a tick is found, remove it with tweezers and clean the area with an antiseptic.

Removing Ticks

A tick usually doesn't bite until it has been attached to your body for 24 hours. So, if a tick should become attached to you, remove it as soon as possible:

- Use tweezers to pull the tick straight away from the skin.
- Grasp the tick by the head with the tweezers.
- Do not twist or jerk ticks, as mouth parts may be left in the skin.
- Do not use a hot match or cigarette to remove a tick. This may cause the tick to burst.
- Avoid touching ticks with bare hands.
- After removing a tick, carefully disinfect the bite site. Wash hands with soap and water.

Review These Important Points

- Whenever bitten, try to identify the tick to help doctors diagnose the trouble.
- Lyme disease can cause a bulls-eye rash that is more than two inches in diameter.
- Remove leaves, tall grass, and brush from work areas. This will reduce tick, deer, and rodent habitat.

Topic:		
Instructor:	Location:	
Printed Name	**Signature**	**Date**

Topic: Tree Pruning and Ladder Safety

Before workers begin working from ladders to prune trees, they should be properly trained. Landscape maintenance crews should include an experienced person to simplify and expedite ladder moving. Moving ladders can cause extra work and may lead to additional accidents.

Tripod Ladders

Tripod ladders are designed for soft and uneven terrain. With three legs, they offer the greatest stability. They lack spreaders, locking devices, steel points, and safety shoes. The top of the ladder can be made of a combination of wood or metal. Tripod ladders have these features:

- Single back leg provides relatively stable support on uneven terrain.
- Steps are at least 27 inches long and should have a metal angle brace.
- Maximum flare on the top to bottom rails (averaging 2-1/4 inches per foot) is required to stabilize the base.
- A wide foot on the rails is provided to control excessive penetration in soft soil.

Improper setup and use of tripod ladders leads to many accidents, including falls:

- The top of a ladder is not a step and should never be used as a step.
- Only one person should be on the ladder at a time.
- This ladder is not a general-purpose ladder and should only be used by a landscape maintenance crew for pruning operations.
- The back of a tripod ladder should be towards the center of the tree or shrub, allowing for additional support if the worker slips.

Closed Top Ladders

A closed-top ladder has two rails that come together at the top. This closed top makes for an easy fit into a tree limb crotch. The closed top also increases stability. Workers should be sure that the closed top fits securely into the tree limb crotch.

Step Ladder

- Be sure the spreader is locked before you climb on the ladder.
- Never stand on the top or the top step of a stepladder.

Extension and Straight Ladders

- Extension and straight ladders can be safe for tree pruning with optional equipment:
  - Steel spikes to keep the base from slipping/skidding.
  - Rubber sleeves on the upper rail sector to reduce branch abrasion and the possibility of slippage along the tree limb.
- Make sure the base of the ladder is level and firmly placed on the ground. Use the four-to-one rule for proper positioning.

- Secure the top of the ladder to the tree so it allows access above the branch being cut. Allow for any upward movement of the branch once the branch is cut.
- Never stand on the top three rungs of an extension or straight ladder.
- Always face the ladder and hold onto the side rails with both hands when going up or down.
- Use a safety rope to raise and lower tools.
- Keep your body centered between the rails of the ladder while working.
- Never use a ladder in a strong wind.
- Consider using a full-body harness or safety belt.

Overhead Electrical Hazards
- **Check for overhead power lines!**
- Stay at least 10 feet away from power lines.
- If you work near electrical power lines, always use a wooden or fiberglass ladder. Never use a metal ladder around power lines.

Review These Important Points
- Tripod ladders are a source of accidents.
- The top of the ladder is not a step.
- The back of a tripod ladder should be aimed toward the tree or shrub center.
- Everyone using a ladder should have proper training before work begins.

Topic:		
Instructor:	Location:	
Printed Name	**Signature**	**Date**

Topic: Tree Pruning, Trimming, and Felling Safety

Pruning, trimming, and felling trees are risky because:
- Workers can fall.
- Workers can come into contact with overhead power lines.
- Workers are using loud and dangerous tools like chain saws.
- Falling limbs or trees can strike workers or by-standers on the ground.

Tree climbing using rope systems can be more risky than working from a bucket truck or aerial lift due to:
- Unstable work position.
- Weakness of ropes to damage from equipment such as chain saws.
- Physical fatigue from using ropes.

General Safety Tips for Tree Pruning, Trimming, and Felling
- **Check for overhead power lines!**
- Inform co-workers and neighbors in the vicinity.
- If a ladder is used, tie it to the tree and use a ladder to have access above the branch.
- Use a fall-arrest harness attached to a secure part of the tree.
- Use warning signs around the work site to prevent public access.
- Use control lines on trees, to direct their fall in the intended direction.
- When felling, keep a distance of at least twice the length of the tree between the tree and people.
- Have a co-worker assist in controlling movement of falling branches.
- Stay at least 10 feet away from power lines
- Use an observer to watch out for power lines.
- Safety observer should wear protective clothing.
- All workers and observers should wear hard hat, goggles, hearing protection, fluorescent vest, cut-resistant trousers, and safety boots.

Review These Important Points
- Use warning signs and barricades around the work site to prevent public access.
- Wear hard hat, goggles, hearing protection, fluorescent vest, cut-resistant trousers, and safety boots.
- Have a co-worker assist in controlling movement of falling branches.
- Use an observer to watch out for power lines.

Topic:		
Instructor:	Location:	

Printed Name	Signature	Date

Topic: Wood Chippers and Shredders Safety

The knives on wood chippers and shredders are sharp enough to slice through fresh wood. The engines are powerful enough to grind thick branches and limbs. Those same knives and engines would make short work of a worker's finger, a hand, or an arm. Workers can be pulled into the knives or struck by the chipper disc hood. Workers should never operate this equipment without training.

Hazards of Wood Chippers and Shredders

- Workers feeding materials into self-feeding chippers or shredders can get caught in chipper knives. A worker's limb can be shredded.
- An unlatched, improperly secured, or damaged hood can be thrown from the chipper or shredder. Fixtures can easily be thrown if they come into contact with the rotating knives.

Safety Tips for Selecting the Work Area

- Position the chipper or shredder so that workers do not have to stand on slopes when feeding material into the machine.
- Keep the area around the chipper or shredder free of tripping hazards.
- Put up warning signs to keep the public a safe distance from work area.
- Ensure that the dislodging chute is positioned to prevent chips from being blown in any direction.

Safety Precautions for Knives

- Wear a hard hat, sturdy slip-resistant footwear, eye protection, hearing protection, gloves without cuffs, and pants without cuffs.
- Keep shirt sleeves buttoned and shirts tucked into pants.
- Read the operator's manual and complete training on proper use and safety precautions before using a chipper or a shredder.
- Do not work alone when using a chipper or a shredder.
- Test all safety and emergency shut-off devices before operating the chipper or the shredder.
- Make sure the material to be chipped is free from stones, metal, and other foreign objects.

Safety Precautions for Disc and Drum Hoods

- If the machine is out of order, tag it with a DO NOT USE tag. If possible, lock it out.
- Make sure that the hood covering the knives is completely closed.
- Run the machine at the lowest possible speed and listen for noises that might indicate broken parts.
- If you hear unusual noises, shut down the machine right away. Have it repaired by a qualified technician.
- Allow all internal machine parts to come to a complete stop before opening the hood covering the disc or drum.
- Wear gloves when handling the knives.
- Knives must be changed if damaged.
- When sharpened knives are fitted, maintain the clearance between the knives and the anvil.

Review These Important Points

- Keep the area around the chipper or the shredder free of tripping hazards.
- Make sure that the hood covering the knives is completely closed.
- Knives must be changed if damaged.

Topic:		
Instructor:	Location:	
Printed Name	**Signature**	**Date**